T0104073

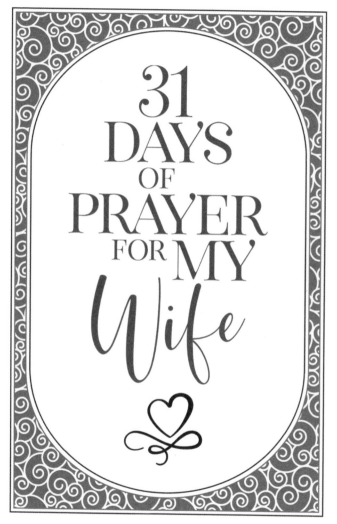

31 DAYS OF PRAYER FOR MY Wife

BroadStreet
PUBLISHING

BroadStreet Publishing Group, LLC
Savage, Minnesota, USA
BroadStreetPublishing.com

31 DAYS OF PRAYER FOR MY *Wife*

Copyright © 2018 Great Commandment Network

978-1-4245-6569-6 faux leather
978-1-4245-5598-7 softcover
978-1-4245-5599-4 e-book

All rights reserved. No part of this book may be reproduced in any form, except for brief quotations in printed reviews, without permission in writing from the publisher.

Unless otherwise indicated, all Scripture is taken from the Holy Bible, New Living Translation, copyright © 1996, 2004, 2007 by Tyndale House Foundation. Used by permission of Tyndale House Publishers, Inc., Carol Stream, Illinois 60188, USA. All rights reserved. Scripture quotations marked NIV are taken from the Holy Bible, New International Version®, NIV® Copyright ©1973, 1978, 1984, 2011 by Biblica, Inc.® Used by permission. All rights reserved worldwide. Scripture quotations marked ESV are taken from The Holy Bible, English Standard Version. Copyright © 2000; 2001 by Crossway Bibles, a division of Good News Publishers. Used by permission. All rights reserved. Scripture quotations marked NASB are taken from the New American Standard Bible, © Copyright 1960, 1962, 1963, 1968, 1971, 1972, 1973, 1975, 1977 by The Lockman Foundation. Used by permission. Scripture quotations marked MSG are from THE MESSAGE. Copyright © by Eugene H. Peterson 1993, 1994, 1995, 1996, 2000, 2001, 2002. Used by permission of NavPress Publishing Group. Scripture quotations marked TPT are from The Passion Translation®. Copyright © 2014, 2015, 2016 by Passion & Fire Ministries, Inc. Used by permission. All rights reserved. the PassionTranslation.com. Scripture quotations marked NKJV are taken from the New King James Version. Copyright © 1982 by Thomas Nelson, Inc. Used by permission. All rights reserved. Scripture quotations marked HCSB® are taken from the Holman Christian Standard Bible®, copyright © 1999, 2000, 2002, 2003, 2009 by Holman Bible Publishers. Used by permission. HCSB® is a federally registered trademark of Holman Bible Publishers.

Typesetting and design by Garborg Design Works | garborgdesign.com
Revised and edited by Michelle Winger | literallyprecise.com

Printed in China

22 23 24 25 5 4 3 2 1

CONTENTS

A SPIRIT-EMPOWERED DISCIPLE
LOVES PEOPLE

A SPIRIT-EMPOWERED DISCIPLE
LIVES HIS MISSION

INTRODUCTION

Marriage is one of the most exciting relationships God has created; yet all marriages could use more of God, more of His Word, and more Christlike attitudes that put each other first. That's why we've written *31 Days of Prayer for My Wife*.

We've served hundreds of thousands of couples with training events and resources, and it's confirmed: every couple wants a strong, intimate, thriving marriage! Too often though, in their search for closeness, many couples find themselves asking the wrong question.

Could it be that an enriched, deepened marriage full of joy, intimacy, and fulfillment is realized not by focusing on and answering the question, "How do I get the most out of my marriage?" but by answering the question, "How does God get what He wants out of my marriage?" Through this resource, we give you a daily opportunity to hear God's perspective about your wife and your marriage. Inviting the Creator of marriage *into* a marriage is always a good idea!

Finally, we've also designed *31 Days of Prayer for My Wife* for your enrichment, encouragement, and growth. As you spend time with Jesus, in His Word, your life will forever be changed.

May God richly bless your time with Jesus and your relationship with your wife.

Terri Snead
Executive Editor, Great Commandment Network

1

The Great Commandment Network is an international collaborative network of strategic kingdom leaders from the faith community, marketplace, education, and caregiving fields who prioritize the powerful simplicity of the words of Jesus to love God, love others, and see others become His followers (Matthew 22:37–40; Matthew 28:19–20).

WHY I SHOULD PRAY FOR MY WIFE

Why is it important to dedicate the time or make it a priority to pray for your wife? Setting aside thirty-one days to pray for her makes sense for many reasons. Here are just a few:

- **As you pray** for your wife, you're joining Jesus as He prays on her behalf.

Hebrews says "He lives forever to intercede with God on [our] behalf" (Hebrews 7:25). In the book of Romans, Paul writes, "he is sitting in the place of honor at God's right hand, pleading for us" (Romans 8:34). Don't you imagine the Savior's prayer list includes your wife? When you pray, you have the privilege of joining Jesus in prayer for her.

- **As you pray for your wife,** you're joining Jesus in His celebrations.

In Christ's last moments on earth, He revealed His loving desire for His followers: "that my joy may be in you, and that your joy may be made full" (John 15:11 NASB). Jesus finds joy in your wife and in your marriage. Since marriage is a special representation of Christ's love for the church, Jesus feels an exceptional joy when He sees marriages thriving. He loves when your relationship is a testimony to a hurting world. When you pray, you have the privilege of joining Jesus in a celebration of the beauty of marriage. (See Proverbs 18:22; James 1:17.)

- **As you pray for your wife**, you're joining Jesus in His concern.

Jesus feels compassion for the struggles in your marriage and any challenges your wife might be facing. His heart is moved with compassion when He sees your bride hurting, disappointed, discouraged, or alone. So join Jesus in praying for her, lifting up concerns and asking the Lord to give you a deeper understanding of your wife. Praying for her allows the Holy Spirit to help you see what He sees, so you can love her the way that Jesus loves. (See 2 Corinthians 1:2–4.)

- **As you pray for your wife**, you strengthen your own walk with Jesus.

Spending time with your Savior deepens your closeness with Him. As you pray, the Spirit will minister to your heart, to your needs, and to your concerns. So, pray for your wife! Pray often. Pray consistently. Pray boldly. And pray faithfully. (See Romans 8:26–27.)

Take the next few moments and join Jesus in prayer.

* Jesus, when I imagine that I can join you in prayer, my heart feels grateful because _____.

* I want to join you in prayer for my wife. First, I'm grateful *for* my wife because _____.

* I lift up my wife to you and pray specifically that you would _____.

Day 2

HOW TO PRAY
FOR MY WIFE

A world in which the prince of darkness seeks to steal, kill, and destroy, needs Christ-followers who walk in the light (John 10:10; 12:35 NASB). For the next thirty-one days, be encouraged to take a journey of walking in the light. During your times of prayer, you will walk in the light of God's Son, God's Word, and God's people (John 8:12; Matthew 5:14; Psalm 119:105). As you take the journey, you will spend moments in personal prayer and in prayer for your wife. You'll pray for her to

- encounter Jesus in fresh, new ways,
- live out the Bible frequently, and
- interact with people in supportive, practical ways.

Have a first encounter with Jesus. As you read these words from the Savior, imagine that He is speaking directly to you. Listen for His compassionate, strong voice. He's thrilled to share these moments just with you.

PRAY: LISTEN TO JESUS

The darkness of this world is all around you, and I don't want you to be overtaken. So I have a plan. I have a plan for your protection, guidance, and strength. If you'll spend time with me, my Word, and my people, darkness won't have a chance. As you encounter me, I will protect you because I'm the Light of the World. Let my Word guide you and light your way. Let my people encourage you and give you strength. Walking in the light is the best place to be because that means we're walking together. (See John 8:12; Matthew 5:14; Psalm 119:105.)

* Jesus, when I look at the darkness of this world, I feel especially concerned about _____.

* Lord, I am grateful for your protection, guidance, and strength, particularly because _____.

* Jesus, I pray that my wife would spend more quality time with you, your Word, and your people, so darkness doesn't have a chance in our home or in our marriage.

* I pray you would protect my wife from _____.

* I pray you would guide my wife in _____.

* I pray you would strengthen my wife in _____.

As you continue this journey of prayer, remember the goal. Your times of prayer can't be focused on changing your wife. These moments with Jesus and His Word are designed to first develop Christlikeness in you. The destination of your journey is a person, and His name is Jesus. As you spend time focused on getting to know Christ and experiencing more of His love, and as you spend time living out His Word, not just reading or hearing it, you'll become like Him. This journey will change something—and hopefully it's you!

Finally, as you take this journey of prayer, it will also be important to remember this goal: your wife doesn't need more things to do or more assessments of her behavior. She rarely needs to hear more information or rational advice. She will change as she encounters Jesus, His Word, and His people.

You may be thinking, *My wife needs to change in some areas. Our marriage needs to be stronger in specific ways. If I can't give advice or information or assessment, what can I do?*

Pray. Have your own encounters with Jesus and see what changes He might want to make in you.

Live. Consistently live out God's Word and do the Bible in your home and marriage. Watch His Word make a difference.

Act. Use the ideas from this resource and take action steps. Take initiative to love your wife in practical, relevant ways.

Pray, live, and act. Then watch the power of God's Son, His Word, and His people make a difference in your wife and in your marriage.

Day 3

WHAT TO PRAY
FOR MY WIFE

This book is designed to foster your Spirit-empowered faith—a faith that is demonstrable, observable, and only possible with the empowerment of the Holy Spirit. A framework for this kind of spiritual growth has been drawn from a cluster analysis of several Greek and Hebrew words that declare that Christ's followers are to be equipped for works of ministry or service. (See Ephesians 4:12.) Therefore, in this book you'll find specific sections that are designed around four themes. (See Appendix 3.) A Spirit-empowered disciple:

- **Loves the Lord** by talking to and listening to God for daily decisions and direction for life (Luke 10:38–42). You will find seven days of prayer marked L-2.

- **Lives the Word** by demonstrating a love for God's Word and living it out every day (2 Corinthians 3:2). You will find seven days of prayer marked W-2.

- **Loves People** by discerning relational needs of others and sharing God's love in meaningful ways (Ephesians 4:29). You will find seven days of prayer marked P-3.

- **Lives His Mission** by actively sharing their lives with others and telling them about the Jesus who lives inside of them (1 Thessalonians 2:8). You will find seven days of prayer marked M-1.

The world needs couples living as Spirit-empowered disciples who are making disciples who, in turn, make more disciples. Thus, this book rightly focuses on the powerful simplicity of

- loving God as your first priority,
- living His Word because there's power and possibility in experiencing Scripture,
- loving people by developing a lifestyle of giving first to your wife and then to others around you, and
- living His mission, which means building a lasting legacy.

After three days of prayer focused on why, how, and what to pray for your wife, you will turn your attention to specific prayer themes. Before you focus on these thematic prayers, live out God's Word. God says that if you ask anything according to His will, He hears you and grants your request (1 John 5:14–15). You know it's His will for you to love your wife well, so you can count on Him to grant this request. Spend the next few moments in prayer. Make your request to God and look for how He gives to you: "If you ask the Father for anything in My name, He will give it to you" (John 16:23 NASB).

LIVE: DO THE BIBLE

God, I know it's your will for me to love my wife well, so I'm asking you to give me whatever I need to do that. If I need to change, show me. If I need to see things differently, I'm ready. I'm asking these things in your name, knowing that you will answer my prayer and give me what I ask. In Jesus' name. Amen.

Notes

A SPIRIT-EMPOWERED DISCIPLE

Loves the Lord

PRAYING TOGETHER

Talk to and listen to God for your daily decisions and direction for life, especially in regard to your spiritual closeness.

STORIES FROM A HUSBAND'S HEART

The mystery of two becoming one in marriage is only possible through an intimate relationship with the One who ordained it. Prayer is the avenue of relationship with the Author of marriage. Marriage was intended to live out of mutual, divine dependency.

As my wife and I go to the Lord in prayer and depend upon Him to relieve any suffering, comfort any pain, or meet any need, He provides an unlimited source of love for each of us. Prayer acknowledges our absolute dependency upon God and draws upon Him as the source of abundant love.

We have also discovered that prayer brings humility to our relationship and increases compassion for each other. As I pray with my wife, I am reminded of my own need for forgiveness and grace. As we pray together about issues with the kids or decisions in our careers, I am challenged to humbly acknowledge my inadequacies and submit myself to God's unmerited favor.

Finally, we have found benefit in this simple prayer: "Lord, I want what you want. Help me discern it and give me power to live it." Regardless of the issue or the conflict, as we pray this type of prayer together, we experience oneness in our desire to know and do His will.

PRAY: LISTEN TO JESUS

I long to have quiet moments of conversation with you and your wife. I love when you are still and free of distractions because those are the times when you can truly feel my love. I especially enjoy seeing you pray together as a couple. When the three of us come together in prayer, miraculous things can happen. Remember, I am the God of love. So it's in these quiet moments of time with me that I can be your unlimited source of love. (See Psalm 46:10; 1 John 4:8.)

* Jesus, I ask that you quiet my mind and spirit. Help me to focus on you. In my relationship with my wife, I am depending on you to _____. Since you are the God of love, I am counting on you to _____.

* Lord, I pray for my wife. Would you draw her closer to you? Since you are the God of love, I ask that you empower her to _____.

LIVE: DO THE BIBLE

Are any of you suffering hardships? You should pray.

—JAMES 5:13

* God, I come to you now about the hardships I am enduring. I need to know that you care about _____. Please reassure me of your love. I need you to intervene in this situation because _____. I am depending on you to _____.

* God, in the same way, I pray for my wife. She needs to know that you care about _____. Please reassure her of your love. She needs you to intervene in this situation: _____. I am depending on you to _____.

TAKE ACTION

• Invite your wife to talk with you about the spiritual goals you both have (e.g., more times of prayer together, Bible study, devotionals, church attendance, etc.). Implement one of these ideas this week.

• Invite your wife to join you as you lead out in prayer. Spend several minutes discussing the most pressing needs and hardships of your life together and then pray.

CLAIM HIS PROMISES

Come near to God and he will come near to you.

—JAMES 4:8 NIV

Love the Lord L-2:
A Spirit-empowered disciple listens to and hears God for daily decisions and direction for life.

Day 5

CELEBRATE YOUR DIFFERENCES

Talk to and listen to God for your daily decisions and direction for life, especially as you navigate the ways in which you are different.

STORIES FROM A HUSBAND'S HEART

My wife and I have wasted a lot of time arguing over whose ways are better. We've fought over every imaginable issue: "There's no money in the account," "There's no gas in my car," and "Why didn't you call and tell me they were coming home with you?" We've been slow learners at times, but we've found a better way.

Here's the way we now handle our differing perspectives: We begin with the principle that neither of us has thoughts, ideas, plans, or ways that are always best. We've learned to navigate the challenges of differing perspectives by prayerfully asking the Lord to show us His thoughts on the matter. Since His thoughts are higher than ours, we know His ways are best. And as we've learned to approach the challenges of marriage in this way, we've not only enjoyed more harmony, but we've also come to appreciate one another's perspective. I've come to value my wife's insight into people, her sensitivity to our kids' needs, and her gift of hospitality.

She's come to more fully appreciate my attention to detail, persistence in completing projects, and vision for our financial future.

PRAY: LISTEN TO JESUS

Humble yourself, and I will lift you up. I love it when you acknowledge your dependence on me. I can't wait to come to your aid. I am ready to teach you my ways and lead you in how to celebrate the differences between you and your wife. Your humility is what moves me to action. I keep my distance from the proud. So talk freely about how you need me and are depending on me. (See James 4:10; Psalm 25:9; 69:32; 138:6; Isaiah 55:8; 1 Peter 3:7.)

* Jesus, please show me your ways and your thoughts. Especially when I'm tempted to think that my ways are best, reveal your perspective. I need to specifically hear you concerning _____.

* Lord, I pray for my wife and our marriage. We are depending on you to help us navigate our differences. We especially need your help concerning _____.

LIVE: DO THE BIBLE

We are God's masterpiece. He has created us anew in Christ Jesus, so we can do the good things he planned for us long ago.
—EPHESIANS 2:10

* God, I want to see my wife as your masterpiece. Show me the traits about her that make you particularly proud of your creation. Show me, Lord. I am celebrating these unique characteristics about my wife: _____.

* God, in the same way, I pray that my wife would see me as a unique creation of yours. Bring unity in our relationship, particularly in how we _____.

* Lord, you have planned good things for each of us to do. Increase our unity and help us celebrate our differences, so we might point more and more people to you.

TAKE ACTION

• If you have a question or concern about your wife's decisions, lovingly discuss it in private.

• Write down the improvements or changes that you could make that would help your marriage communication, especially regarding the ways you are different.

• Look for an opportunity to defer to your wife. Say something like, "We're really different in this area, and yet I want to give to you by _____."

CLAIM HIS PROMISES

You faithfully answer our prayers with awesome deeds, O God our savior.

—Psalm 65:5

Love the Lord L-2:
A Spirit-empowered disciple listens to and hears God for daily decisions and direction for life.

Day 6

GOALS AND
PLANS

Talk to and listen to God for your daily decisions and direction for life, especially in regard to goals for your future.

STORIES FROM A HUSBAND'S HEART

The intimacy in our marriage increased and our overall relationship improved when we began what we called "marriage staff meetings." These weekly times to talk made all the difference. For a while, we had lunch together every Thursday. At other times, we met on Tuesday nights after the kids were asleep. We made this time a priority, and it paid off.

One of the most special benefits that came out of our marriage staff meetings was our ability to plan and accomplish goals for our future. We felt safe enough to talk about our financial goals and what we wanted to do when the kids were grown. We discussed plans for improving our home, and projects we wanted to get done in the yard. We planned our date nights and family vacations. These discussions increased our unity and helped us accomplish the goals that were important to both of us.

PRAY: LISTEN TO JESUS

I love to see the plans you make, especially as you include me. It brings me joy to give you the desires of your heart and make your plans succeed. It's a part of my divine nature to bring good things to your life. So seek me out, include me in your plans, because I long to meet your needs.

Harmony is precious to me, beloved. I love seeing my people make decisions in unity. If you're having trouble, remember that the Holy Spirit is interceding on your behalf. He's praying for you and your wife. His prayers are meant to help you live according to my will. (See Matthew 6:33; Psalm 20:4, 133:2; Romans 8:27.)

* Jesus, I know you have good things planned for us, and I'm grateful. You've been faithful to give us _____. Grant us wisdom now as we make plans to _____.

* Lord, I pray that my wife and I would come together in harmony around these goals: _____. Thank you that your Spirit is interceding for us about _____.

LIVE: DO THE BIBLE

I will seek the one I love.

—Song of Solomon 3:2

* God, I want to seek your counsel about this goal: _____. Help me to know the best way and best time to seek my wife's input about our plans for _____.

* God, in the same way, I pray that my wife would hear from you about _____. Show us the plans you have for us. We want to hear what you have to say about _____. Bring us to unity, Lord. We want to please you with the harmony of our marriage.

TAKE ACTION

* Ask your wife to discuss plans for a special date night. Meet your goal for increased closeness.

* Ask your wife's input about the specific character traits that need to be emphasized as you train each of your children. Discuss plans for parenting in these ways.

* Write down your response to this statement: "If all my dreams for the future could come true, here's what our life, marriage, and family would look like: _____." Ask your wife to do the same, and then talk through both responses.

CLAIM HIS PROMISES

For I know the plans I have for you, says the Lord. They are plans for good and not for evil, to give you a future and a hope.

—JEREMIAH 29:11 TLB

Love the Lord L-2:
A Spirit-empowered disciple listens to and hears God for daily decisions and direction for life.

ATTITUDE
OF GRATITUDE

Talk to and listen to God for your daily decisions and direction for life.
Cultivate a spirit of gratitude and thanksgiving.

STORIES FROM A HUSBAND'S HEART

Last Christmas, I was struck by a simple statement of gratitude in
the story of Jesus. God lovingly provided Mary with a special relationship in Elizabeth. The Lord knew Mary would need the blessing
of another human who understood the incredible, divinely orches-
trated circumstances. The most blessed of all women expressed
gratitude because she wasn't going through the circumstances
alone: "My soul exalts the Lord" (Luke 1:46 NASB). As I read those
words, I was amazed. Mary's gratitude wasn't about her position,
but about relationship.

I now see that the same God who blessed Mary with a special
relationship has sent my wife as one of His most special gifts for me.
God has provided a beautiful wife for me, and she is a blessing from

Him (Proverbs 18:22). More and more frequently, I've recognized a sense of deep gratitude for her. She has seen my less-than-perfect side and still accepts me, her strengths lovingly balance my weaknesses, and she thinks of me, gives to me, and cares about me. She's the partner and blessing my God has given to me. Because of this, my soul exalts the Lord.

PRAY: LISTEN TO JESUS

In case you're unsure of how to connect with me, I've given you a hint. Thank me. I've given you everything you enjoy— every breath you breathe and every relationship you call dear. It's my absolute joy to give, yet it hurts my heart when the ones I love forget to say thank you. I feel loved and honored when I hear your words of gratitude. My followers who have learned to acclaim me walk in my presence and find great blessing. Your gratitude keeps us close. (See Psalm 50:23, 69:30, 89:15; 1 Thessalonians 5:18.)

* Jesus, I don't ever want you to feel disappointed because I forget to say thank you. When I imagine how much you have given to me and my family, and how you might experience hurt because of my lack of gratitude, I feel _____.

* Lord, I don't want to forget to say thank you for my wife. She is a gift from you. Remind me of all the ways she is a special blessing from you to me. Keep me from being critical. I'm grateful you found and provided her for me because _____.

LIVE: DO THE BIBLE

I will praise God's name with singing,
and I will honor him with thanksgiving.

—PSALM 69:30

* God, I want to bring you honor with my gratitude. Remind me of some of the special ways you have loved me recently. Today, I am particularly grateful for these ten things: _____.

* God, in the same way, I pray for my wife. Move her heart with gratefulness for how you have loved her well. I want her to enjoy the blessing of walking in your presence. I want her to receive the joy of special connection with you because _____.

TAKE ACTION

• Tell your wife some of the ways that she is a blessing to you. Share the top ten reasons she is God's gift.

• Brag about your wife and how you've been blessed by her. Share a post on social media or find some other public way to demonstrate your gratitude. Brag in front of your kids, family members, or friends: "I've recently been reminded of some of the great qualities in my wife. I'm grateful God gave her to me because _____."

CLAIM HIS PROMISES

Giving thanks is a sacrifice that truly honors me.
If you keep to my path,
I will reveal to you the salvation of God.

—PSALM 50:23

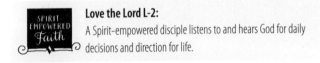

Love the Lord L-2:
A Spirit-empowered disciple listens to and hears God for daily decisions and direction for life.

Day 8

A STUDENT
OF MY WIFE

Talk to and listen to God for your daily decisions and direction for life, especially as you live out the kindness of the Lord.

STORIES FROM A HUSBAND'S HEART

I've learned that I need to be a student of my wife. It's a lifelong pursuit of understanding and knowing her, so I can love her well. The Lord knew I would need a lot of help when He reminded me to live with my wife in an understanding way. I'll never figure her out without His help (see 1 Peter 3:7 NASB).

Here are just some of the things I've learned about my wife. I know not to buy her flowers or candy; she prefers more practical gifts. I know the colors she likes and her favorite brands of clothing and jewelry. I know she likes to socialize but not stay out too late. I know she prefers me to drive, but with caution. I know she likes to people watch, shop, and drink coffee, but will drink only decaf after five o'clock in the evening.

As the Lord increases my understanding of my wife, He then invites and empowers me to demonstrate His kindness. He is wonderfully patient and kind with me. I get to pay His kindness forward to my wife.

LISTEN TO JESUS

Remember, my beloved. I am wonderfully kind, patient, and tolerant of you. It was my kindness, in spite of your sin, that first drew you into a relationship with me. Now I'm giving you the opportunity to share some of that kindness with your wife. Pay it forward every day. Look for ways to demonstrate kindness with her. Be generous as I am generous. Take thought of her just as I think of you a thousand times a day. Finally, remember that sharing truth is important, but that it needs to be coupled with kindness. (See Romans 2:4; Proverbs 3:3; Ephesians 4:15; Psalm 139:17.)

* Jesus, you are so right. You have been patient, kind, and tolerant of me even though I _____. I am grateful for your kindness toward me because _____. I pray that you would empower me to demonstrate this same kindness in my marriage. I need your help to _____.

* Lord, I pray that my wife would have a fresh experience with your kindness as well. May she sense your patience and understanding and the generous way you love us both. I pray specifically that she would sense your kindness related to _____.

LIVE: DO THE BIBLE

Be kind to each other, tenderhearted, forgiving one another,
just as God through Christ has forgiven you.

—EPHESIANS 4:32

* God, remind me often of my wife's preferences and uniquenesses. Show me the things I need to understand about her. Based on these special things, show me ways I can demonstrate your kindness. Show me how to be tenderhearted with her. Show me any areas where I need to forgive, just as you've forgiven me. Speak to me, Lord. I'm listening for _____.

* Lord, I pray for my wife. Give her a fresh experience of your kindness and tenderness. I want her to soak in your forgiveness. Show her more and more of the ways she is loved by you so that _____.

TAKE ACTION

• Give your wife an unexpected, no-strings-attached hug, back rub, or foot massage.

• Serve your wife her favorite meal.

• Compliment your wife on her appearance.

• Praise your wife for an accomplishment or achievement.

CLAIM HIS PROMISES

Those who are kind benefit themselves,
but the cruel bring ruin on themselves.

—PROVERBS 11:17 NIV

Love the Lord L-2:
A Spirit-empowered disciple listens to and hears God for daily decisions and direction for life.

Day 9

HOPE INTO FAITH

Talk to and listen to God for your daily decisions and direction for life.
Learn how to turn hope into faith.

STORIES FROM A HUSBAND'S HEART

My constant desire to work has often caused conflict between my wife and me. After a decade of marriage, we noticed a dilemma. She saw my workaholic tendencies as me making a priority of my plans, goals, dreams, and agenda. I saw my work as important and vital because it provided for our family. She hoped I would work less. I hoped she would stop fussing at me so I could keep my job. We were at an impasse.

After getting counsel from one of our mentors, we came to see this impasse as an opportunity to turn our hope into faith. Our mentor challenged me to live out Philippians 2:3 and think more highly of my wife and kids than I did myself. As I thought more highly of others, I could trust God to get the work done. He was faithful. Work got done and harmony returned to our home. Our mentor challenged my wife to live out Ephesians 4:15 and speak the truth in love. Instead of verbal attacks, she learned to say, "You've been working hard this week, but I've really missed you. Could we plan some time just for us?" As she lived out this principle, her hopes turned into faith. She relied on the Holy Spirit to use these gentle words to change my heart.

God's Word works. We just have to live it.

PRAY: LISTEN TO JESUS

Trust me completely, then look for how I will provide. I am your security; you can count on my faithfulness. My faithfulness is as enduring as the heavens. Your demonstration of faith in me makes my heart sing. There are great blessings in store for the ones who put their faith in me: the faith-filled receive my protection, my favor, and a place of undeserved privilege. Place your faith in me and my Word and watch the things you hope for come into reality. (See Philippians 4:19; Proverbs 2:8, 3:26; Psalm 89:2; Matthew 8:10; Romans 5:2; Hebrews 11:1, 6.)

* Jesus, I want to please you, so I am trusting you in this area of my life: _____. I'm trusting you in this area of my marriage: _____. Please show me in your Word, how the things I hope for can be turned into demonstrations of faith in you (see Romans 15:4).

* Lord, I also pray that my wife would have a fresh sense of your faithfulness. I pray she would feel your protection and your favor as she puts her trust in you. Empower her to put her faith in you, especially regarding _____.

LIVE: DO THE BIBLE

Faith shows the reality of what we hope for; it is the evidence of things we cannot see.

—Hebrews 11:1

* God, as I consider my relationship with my wife, I am hoping for _____. Because I know that my faith pleases you, I am counting on you to _____.

* Lord, I ask that you would give my wife the same vision. I know she is hoping for _____ as it relates to our life together. Please reveal how she might demonstrate more faith in you, so she can please you.

TAKE ACTION

* Ask your wife what she is hoping for in your marriage. Seek the Lord's wisdom for how to make those changes.

* Memorize specific Bible promises that you are longing to see happen.

CLAIM HIS PROMISES

"If you have faith the size of a mustard seed, you will tell this mountain, 'Move from here to there,' and it will move. Nothing will be impossible for you."

—Matthew 17:20 hcsb

Love the Lord L-2:

A Spirit-empowered disciple listens to and hears God for daily decisions and direction for life.

Day 10

UNWRAPPING YOUR GIFTS

Talk to and listen to God for your daily decisions and direction for life, and especially about your gifts.

STORIES FROM A HUSBAND'S HEART

When our son was about five years old, he went through a tremendous fear of separation. My wife and I struggled with how to love him through this challenging time. What we quickly realized is that I needed to love my wife through this stage as well. She vulnerably shared her perspective with me one day: "I think God wants me to come to a place where I trust Him to protect our kids. For too long, I've operated with a perspective that says, 'God gave us these kids, but I'm the only one who can be counted on to protect them.'"

God had to do a significant work in my wife and in me. First, we made a plan to slowly encourage our son to separate from us. We took small steps that encouraged him to stay with others. We left him with grandparents for a few hours, then for the evening and eventually overnight. Slowly God began to restore his sense of security.

More importantly though, I learned to reassure my wife of my love. We prayed together for God to reassure her heart; together we sensed the importance of trusting God's loving protection for our family and our kids. We had many conversations about how God can take care of our kids even better than we can. Our heavenly Father reassured us so that we could reassure our son.

PRAY: LISTEN TO JESUS

There's nothing stronger than a parent's love for his or her child. In fact, I see that love every time our Father looks at you. I also see the joy in your face when you take time to truly see your own children. Children are some of the Father's most precious gifts, so be sure to unwrap and admire them. Parenting is hard, so let me be your provider and guide. Just ask me for help, for I love to give it to you. (See Psalm 25:5, 127:3; Matthew 7:11.)

* Jesus, I want to demonstrate the kind of love you have for me to my children. Remind me often of the Father's love and then help me live that out in my family. Help me lead our family in ways that bring security and peace to our home. I especially need your help in this area: _____.

* Lord, I pray that you would often remind my wife of your love so she is free, empowered by your Spirit, and equipped with your wisdom to parent our kids in the ways they need it most. Our kids need _____, so please give my wife _____.

LIVE: DO THE BIBLE

Children are a gift from God; they are his reward.

—PSALM 127:3 TLB

* Jesus, please help us to unwrap the gifts you have given us. Slow me down so I can truly know them. What about my children do you want me to admire? What do you want me to see about their needs? Their future? How can I come alongside my wife and parent our children well?

* Lord, I pray that you would equip my wife and me to slow down and unwrap each of our children as gifts from you. Give us divine insight into their needs and show us how to love them the way you love us. I pray specifically for my wife as she parents, that she would _____.

TAKE ACTION

• Offer to take over a parenting responsibility that is typically your wife's; give her the night off.

• Ask your wife how you could better support her in parenting the kids. Be open to her input.

CLAIM HIS PROMISES

In the fear of the LORD one has strong confidence,
and his children will have a refuge.

—PROVERBS 14:26 ESV

SPIRIT EMPOWERED *Faith*

Love the Lord L-2:
A Spirit-empowered disciple listens to and hears God for daily decisions and direction for life.

Notes

A SPIRIT-
EMPOWERED
DISCIPLE

*Lives
the Word*

Day 11

CHEERING FOR ONE ANOTHER

Love God's Word and live it out by encouraging others.

STORIES FROM A HUSBAND'S HEART

My wife and I have learned that sometimes marriage partners are often very different, and that can be a good thing! Intense versus laid-back, reflective versus social, thinker versus doer, wait versus react—the list of differences seems endless, and we often miss their purposes.

We've discovered that some of the ways I'm different can actually be an encouragement to my wife during stressful times. My laid-back nature can temper her perfectionism. My tendencies to wait, reflect, and think have encouraged her at times when she was prepared to "Ready, aim, fire!" My positive outlook can be an asset when things seem a little bleak.

When things are hard, I have to be careful to care about her feelings *first* and offer words of compassion like, "Sweetheart, I'm sad

to know you're feeling that way. It hurts me to see you discouraged."
Then after she knows I care, she often needs my encouragement.
That usually sounds something like this: "I know we can do this.
I believe in you, and I believe in us. We've got this! It's going to be
okay. We're in this together." Cheering for my wife has drawn us
closer even when the circumstances could have pulled us apart.

PRAY: LISTEN TO JESUS

*Come to me when you are discouraged or weary. Come closer
to me when life is hard. I can give you rest. While you are in
this world, there will be trouble, but take heart, I have over-
come the troubles of this world. Remember too: I can fill you
with joy and peace in the midst of the hard times. I am able
to give you sufficiency and abundance for everything I have
called you to do.* (See Matthew 11: 28; Romans 15:13; 2 Corinthians 9:8; John 16:33.)

*   Jesus, thank you for being my encourager. I am weary
    at times, in _____, and I need your _____. Sometimes
    it's hard to keep going in _____, so I need your _____.

*   Lord, I also pray that you lift up and encourage my
    wife. Give her rest in _____. Fill her with joy and peace
    in the midst of _____. Give her your sufficiency and
    abundance for _____.

LIVE: DO THE BIBLE

Encourage each other and build each other up, just as you are already doing.

—1 Thessalonians 5:11

* God, show me the areas where my wife might be weary. Show me the ways in which it might be hard for her to keep going. Help me to know exactly what encouragement she needs and how to communicate it. Speak to my heart, I am listening.

* Jesus, I pray for my wife. It seems as if it's hard for her to keep going in this area: _____. Help me build her up and cheer her forward. I think my wife needs to know that I believe she can _____. Help me communicate my encouragement in ways that are meaningful to her.

TAKE ACTION

• Send your wife a note that begins with these words: I know it's hard sometimes. I want you to know that I believe in you and your _____.

• Ask your wife, "How can I best encourage you as you accomplish your goals this week?"

• Take your wife out for dinner. Fill the conversation with lots of reassuring smiles. Ask her what you can do to relieve some of the stress in her life.

CLAIM HIS PROMISES

God is able to make all grace abound to you, so that always having all sufficiency in everything, you may have an abundance for every good deed.

—2 CORINTHIANS 9:8 NASB

Live the Word W-2:
A Spirit-empowered disciple lives the Word by demonstrating a love for God's Word and living it out every day.

Day 12

A DIVINE
COMMODITY

Love God's Word and live it out, especially as you accept others.

STORIES FROM A HUSBAND'S HEART

Because of the differences in our upbringing, when my wife and I married, our expectations clashed like brown shoes with a black tuxedo. I would come home promptly at six o'clock and expect to get the kids fed, bathed, and have their homework done by eight o'clock, when my wife and I would then spend two luxurious hours together before our own bedtime at ten. Life was supposed to be predictable and structured. Looking back, I realize that those expectations were completely unrealistic.

A part of what I love about my wife is her spontaneity and free spirit. She lives in the moment. Life with her is an adventure. Her style of relating is much less structured. Consequently, in the early years of our marriage, I was pretty intolerant. I came to view her seeming lack of routine as absolutely unacceptable. God showed me that this wasn't necessarily her problem. In his gentle voice, He prompted me with these thoughts one day: *Son, could it be that the intolerance you have for your wife has actually become a "plank in your eye"? Don't worry about the speck in hers. Your lack of acceptance is part of the conflict between you.*

I needed this reminder to accept my wife rather than try to change her to be like me.

PRAY: LISTEN TO JESUS

Acceptance is a divine commodity. It's only available from me. You must receive it before you can give it. When my Father allowed me to die in your place, He made a deliberate choice to look beyond your imperfections, inadequacies, and sin to accept you as you are. This unconditional acceptance is permanent. There is nothing you can do to earn it or lose it. Now I see you as one who is favored, righteous, and worth my blessings. (See Romans 5:8, 15:7; Psalm 5:12; Numbers 6:24–26.)

* Jesus, you loved me and died for me in spite of my _____. I am filled with gratitude for how you have looked beyond my _____. You see me as one who is favored and righteous even though I _____. Help me accept my wife as she is, focusing instead on the changes I need to make.

* Lord, I pray you would reassure my wife of your unconditional acceptance. Confirm to her that your love is not based on her _____. Speak to her heart about how you see her as favored, righteous, and worth your blessings. Let her experience a fresh taste of your acceptance.

LIVE: DO THE BIBLE

Accept each other just as Christ has accepted you so that God will be given glory.

—ROMANS 15:7

* God, I want to accept my wife the way you have accepted me. Show me how you see her. I can sometimes only see our differences, disagreements, irritations, idiosyncrasies, or faults. Help me look beyond those, see her with your eyes, and respond with your love.

* Jesus, I pray that my wife would see me with your eyes. Help her see beyond my faults. Help her sense more of your acceptance and then empower her to give it to others.

TAKE ACTION

* Try this conversation starter. Keep it light-hearted and celebrate your differences: "Remember when we noticed that we were different in _____ ?"

* Write a note to your wife: *I'm grateful that you love me even though I _____.*

* If one of your wife's imperfections shows up, respond with, "We've all got some growing to do. But for me, you're perfect."

CLAIM HIS PROMISES

My grace is sufficient for you, for power is perfected in weakness.

—2 CORINTHIANS 12:9 HCSB

Live the Word W-2:

A Spirit-empowered disciple lives the Word by demonstrating a love for God's Word and living it out every day.

Day 13

TEARS
OF COMFORT

Love God's Word and live it out, especially as you comfort others.

STORIES FROM A HUSBAND'S HEART

The Gospel of John recounts a beautiful example of Christ's compassion. Jesus receives the heartbreaking news that His close friend Lazarus has become very sick. Upon His arrival, Jesus finds Lazarus' sisters, Mary and Martha, mourning the death of their brother. Scripture tells us that when Jesus saw Mary weeping, He was deeply moved and wept openly (John 11:1–35).

It's important to note what Jesus did *not* do when He visited the two sisters. As the Son of God—the One who knew past, present, and future—Jesus certainly knew that Lazarus was going to live again. Christ approached Mary with the full knowledge that He was going to restore their brother's life and set everything as it was. But even though He possessed this knowledge, Jesus didn't give the sisters a pep talk, an explanation, or a sermon on faith. Instead, upon seeing the sadness of their hearts, He wept. The Savior was so moved with compassion for His friends that He shed tears.

That's the kind of comfort needed in marriage. Even if you know a situation will turn out right, you must share in your wife's pain if she is sad or disappointed. Even if you're sure that God will work on your behalf, if your wife is hurting, you must express compassion for the hurt she is enduring.

PRAY: LISTEN TO JESUS

Just as I was moved with compassion for Mary and Martha, I hurt deeply when I see your sadness, disappointment, and hurt. I will never, ever leave you comfortless. My love, comfort, hope, strength, and grace is always available for you. I am the God of all comfort, so when you're called upon to give compassion to others, call on me. (See John 11:1–34, 14:8; 2 Corinthians 1:3–4.)

* Jesus, when I imagine that the Savior of the universe hurts for me, cries for me, and is moved with compassion for me, I feel _____. As I receive your care and comfort, let me share that with my wife when she needs it.

* Lord, I also pray that you would give my wife a personal experience of your divine compassion. I know she's felt hurt about _____ and needs some of your comfort.

LIVE: DO THE BIBLE

Weep with those who weep.

—ROMANS 12:15 NASB

* God, I know that my wife has experienced these hurts, disappointments, and pains: _____. Because I love her, it makes me sad to know that she has gone through these things.

* Jesus, please help me express some of your comfort to my wife. Help me bring healing and comfort to her heart.

TAKE ACTION

- If your wife shares a struggle or painful emotion, listen, sit quietly, and hold her.

- Share words of comfort with your wife:
  - "Sweetheart, I know you have felt _____, and I want you to know that I'm so sorry you're going through this."
  - "It makes me sad to hear you say _____ because I love you and don't want to see you hurting."

CLAIM HIS PROMISES

Show mercy and compassion for others, just as your heavenly Father overflows with mercy and compassion for all.

—LUKE 6:36 TPT

Live the Word W-2:

A Spirit-empowered disciple lives the Word by demonstrating a love for God's Word and living it out every day.

Notes

Day 14

GOOD FOR
THE SOUL

Love God's Word and live it out, especially as we confess our sins to one another.

STORIES FROM A HUSBAND'S HEART

My wife and I were in the kitchen planning our evening. I was going to pick her up after work so we could meet our son for dinner. She said she would be ready at 6:30. Well, because of our past experiences, I just *knew* she would be late, so I told her—very sarcastically—that I'd be there around 7:00. When I left her that morning, I realized I had sinned, and I knew I needed to confess my wrong attitude to God and to my wife.

Most people don't like to confess their mistakes. A lot don't even know how. But confession is simply agreeing with God that some actions, attitudes, or behavior is not in line with His plan.

I first confessed my sin to God and then to my wife. I admitted that my attitude and words were wrong and asked for forgiveness. I didn't enjoy having to confess those things, but I was grateful to

God for helping me keep the lines of communication and intimacy with my wife open.

PRAY: LISTEN TO JESUS

Confession is hard, but it has great reward. Your confession—admitting your wrong actions, attitudes, and behavior—keeps us in right relationship with one another. You have less worry, guilt, and anxiety when you practice confession with me. When you admit your sin, you can count on my forgiveness. It's a promise. Confessing to another person brings the promise of healing in that relationship too. (See 1 John 1:9; Psalm 38:18, 51:1-9; James 5:16; Lamentations 3:23.)

* God, I am grateful for your promise of forgiveness and how that keeps me close to you because _____. Thank you that I can empty my guilt, worry, and anxiety through confession.

* Lord, I pray that you would reassure my wife of your forgiveness. Overwhelm her with the truth that she can trust your lovingkindness to be new every morning.

LIVE: DO THE BIBLE

I acknowledged my sin to You,
and my iniquity I have not hidden.

—PSALM 32:5 NKJV

* God, search my heart and tell me if there are attitudes, behaviors, or habits (especially those that impact my wife) that are wrong in your sight and need my

confession. Lord, I admit that I was wrong in _____.
Forgive me for _____. Help me share these points of
confession with my wife.

* God, I pray for my wife. Empower her to receive my
  confession and forgive. Would you bring more healing
  and restoration to our marriage?

TAKE ACTION

- Set aside a private time with your wife. Share the areas
  of confession that the Lord has revealed.

- Avoid excuses or defensiveness in your confession. A
  great confession sounds like:
    ○ "I was wrong when _____."
    ○ "I know you must have felt _____."
    ○ "Will you forgive me?"

CLAIM HIS PROMISES

Whoever conceals his transgressions will not prosper,
but he who confesses and forsakes them will obtain mercy.

—PROVERBS 28:13 ESV

Live the Word W-2:
A Spirit-empowered disciple lives the Word by demonstrating a
love for God's Word and living it out every day.

Day 15

RELEASE
YOUR GRIP

Love God's Word and live it out, especially as you forgive others.

STORIES FROM A HUSBAND'S HEART

In Greek, the word for forgiveness means "to release." Before, when I forgave, I released the person and the action, but I failed to release my pain. I forgave but I still felt hurt. I wasn't dealing with the pain associated with the offense.

It's been difficult, but I've discovered that I need to share my pain with the Lord. It's not enough just to "gut it out" and forgive my offender. The Lord wants to heal the hurt that I've endured, and that requires that I share it with Him. Jesus wants me to tell Him about my disappointment and let Him comfort me. He wants me to talk with Him about my rejection, so He can remind me He understands how deeply I hurt.

One important step in my experience of forgiveness is to imagine myself alone in the garden of Gethsemane with Jesus. I listen as He shares His hurt and pain with the Father. (See Matthew 26:36–46.) Jesus shared His hurt with God, so it must be okay for me to do the same. I imagine the scene of the angels comforting my suffering Savior (Luke 22:43–44). I'm then free to tell the Father about my own painful experiences and wait until the God of all comfort pours His healing compassion over me. Finally, I reflect on how Jesus must have needed this time of healing and comfort with the Father so that He could offer forgiveness at the cross. In the same way, it is my experience of God's compassion and care that allows me to truly forgive.

PRAY: LISTEN TO JESUS

I am good, ready to forgive, and full of unfailing love for anyone who asks for my help. If someone has hurt you, I want to comfort you and help you forgive. Make allowances for other's faults. Forgive them and you will be forgiven. I know releasing is hard, but it's a matter of stewardship. My Father has granted you forgiveness, now it's your turn to share His gift with others. Remember, if you refuse to forgive, your Father will not forgive you. (See Matthew 6:15; Psalm 86:5; Luke 6:31; Colossians 3:13.)

* Jesus, I need your comfort for my hurt caused by _____. Help me to completely release my pain about _____. Please bring more of your freedom and forgiveness to my life.

* Lord, I pray that you would do the same for my wife. Please remind her of your readiness to help and comfort. Comfort the hurts she has about _____.

LIVE: DO THE BIBLE

Make allowance for each other's faults, and forgive anyone who offends you. Remember, the Lord forgave you, so you must forgive others.

—COLOSSIANS 3:13

* God, just as you have forgiven me, would you help me forgive _____. Help me make allowances for _____. I'm trusting the Holy Spirit to _____.

* Jesus, I pray that you would help my wife forgive _____. Help her make allowances for _____. Empower her to trust your Spirit as _____.

TAKE ACTION

* Write a letter to Jesus, telling Him about the hurts you've experienced and any areas of unforgiveness. Allow the Holy Spirit to bring you comfort, healing, and forgiveness for each moment of pain.

* After you have received comfort from the Lord and have a forgiving heart toward your offender, it may be time to share your hurt. That might sound like: "I need to share something that's been hurtful for me. I care about our relationship and want you to know that it was hurtful when _____ (name the incident without judgment). I felt _____ (name your hurt, not just the anger). Thank you for listening." Then leave the topic, trusting the Holy Spirit to bring confession and change.

CLAIM HIS PROMISES

Love prospers when a fault is forgiven,
but dwelling on it separates close friends.

—PROVERBS 17:9

Live the Word W-2:
A Spirit-empowered disciple lives the Word by demonstrating a love for God's Word and living it out every day.

Day 16

BUILD HER UP

> Love God's Word and live it out, especially as you speak only words that
> edify others.

STORIES FROM A HUSBAND'S HEART

There is an example of edifying one another in the book of Luke.
Jesus was teaching in the temple and saw a widow put two small
coins into the treasury box. He gave the woman an incredible compliment, voicing undeniable approval when He said, "This poor
widow has put in more than all the others. All these people gave
their gifts out of their wealth; but she out of her poverty put in all
she had to live on" (Luke 21:3 NIV).

I was impressed with the Lord's words, but also with His technique.
We don't know if the widow heard the words that Jesus spoke that day,
but we can be sure the disciples and the others at the temple did.

I began to wonder if I should follow the Savior's example and
speak edifying words about my wife to other people. *Should I tell
her mother how I love being her husband? Should I say some affirming words about her in front of her friends—or our children?*

There have been times when I've compared my wife to other
women, times when I have been stingy with praise because I'm

looking at what other wives do for their husbands. The Holy Spirit took me aside that day and began to convict me and remind me to share edifying words with my wife and affirming words about her.

PRAY: LISTEN TO JESUS

When I look at you, I celebrate the specialness of you, my creation. Scripture reveals how I'm generous with my edifying words for you. You are my chosen one. You are my master-piece, the light of the world, holy, blameless, and complete. I want you to have this same view of the people around you. Look for their special qualities and build them up. Think carefully before saying anything that's critical or dishonoring. My followers are careful to only speak words that edify. (See Proverbs 15:28; Ephesians 1:4, 2:10, 4:29; Colossians 1:22.)

* God, I'm grateful for your words of edification for me. Thank you for reminding me that you see me as _____. I'm blessed by the truth that you have called me _____.

* Lord, I pray that my wife would see herself as you see her. Remind her often of the truth that she is _____. Because of your grace, you have called her _____.

LIVE: DO THE BIBLE

Do not let any unwholesome talk come out of your mouths, but only what is helpful for building others up according to their needs, that it may benefit those who listen.

—EPHESIANS 4:29 NIV

* God, make me generous with praise for my wife. What words of edification are most important for her to hear from me? What words of criticism or comparison do I need to get rid of? I want her to only hear words that are honoring.

* Lord, I pray that my wife would live out the command of Ephesians 4:29. Empower her generosity of praise. Give her words that are edifying, not critical or comparative.

TAKE ACTION

• After the Lord has reminded you of the positive character traits that are true of your wife, share those with her privately through a text, note, or verbally. "I'm so proud that you're my wife because of your _____."

• Praise your wife in front of her parents, her friends, or kids. Build her up in public settings.

CLAIM HIS PROMISES

As the bridegroom rejoices over the bride, so your God will rejoice over you.

—ISAIAH 62:5 NIV

Live the Word W-2:
A Spirit-empowered disciple lives the Word by demonstrating a love for God's Word and living it out every day.

Day 17

PRIORITIZING PREFERENCES

Love God's Word and live it out, especially as you give preference to others.

STORIES FROM A HUSBAND'S HEART

For too many years, my wife and I played the waiting game that goes something like this: "I'll do better at giving to your needs after you begin giving to mine." Because of this, we missed out on some of the closeness God wanted for our marriage. Fortunately, God gradually taught us about what it means to give preference to one another.

We tried the exercise below as a way to help us consider one another and then give according to preferences. Here's how it worked. Both of us took a look at this list and checked two or three items that most appealed to us. We had a conversation about our preferences and then focused for the next month on giving to each other based on these preferences. It was revolutionary to our marriage.

☐   Going for a walk together
☐   Being served a favorite meal

- [ ] Getting a back rub or foot massage
- [ ] Being told "I love you"
- [ ] Getting help with errands or chores
- [ ] Being praised for achievements
- [ ] Getting help with the kids
- [ ] Receiving a spontaneous gift
- [ ] Having a quiet conversation
- [ ] Being approached sexually

We learned that our preferences were very different, and that we couldn't wait until our spouse gave first. I learned to give to my wife according to her preferences and then trust that the Lord would move on her heart to give in His timing.

PRAY: LISTEN TO JESUS

Remember, my beloved. I had equal status with my heavenly Father, but I didn't cling to that position. I exchanged my status and the privileges of deity and became human. I did this for you! I gave up myself and gave preference to you and to our relationship. I want this same kind of selflessness to be true of you. Give preference to your wife. Love deeply. Trust in me and I will lift you up. (See Romans 12:10; Philippians 2: 1–11; 1 Peter 5:6.)

* Jesus, I am grateful for your demonstration of humility and how you gave preference to me because _____. I feel _____ when I imagine that you gave up your position in heaven so you could have a relationship with me.

* Lord, I pray that you would plant this same truth deeply into my wife's heart. Give her a fresh experience of how

you have sacrificed and given yourself up for her. I pray specifically that she would sense your _____.

LIVE: DO THE BIBLE

Give preference to one another in honor.

—ROMANS 12:10 NASB

* God, I want to give preference to my wife. Show me the ways I can give myself up for her. Speak to me, Lord, about how I can give up my agenda, preferences, and privileges. Help me do this with a positive attitude and servant spirit.

* Lord, I pray that my wife would sense this same need. Move her heart with this same stewardship and servant's heart. You gave up yourself for us, and we are now called to do the same for others.

TAKE ACTION

• Ask your wife about her preferences from the list above. Discuss those preferences and then focus on your giving. Trust the Lord to meet your needs through your wife in His timing and in His ways.

• Ask your wife to share her responses to this statement: "In our marriage, I would prefer more or less _____. It would mean a lot to me if we could _____."

CLAIM HIS PROMISES

Do nothing out of selfish ambition or vain conceit. Rather, in humility value others above yourselves.

—PHILIPPIANS 2:3 NIV

Live the Word W-2:
A Spirit-empowered disciple lives the Word by demonstrating a love for God's Word and living it out every day.

Notes

Notes

A SPIRIT-
EMPOWERED
DISCIPLE

Loves

People

Day 18

STAMP OF APPROVAL

Discern the relational needs of others and share God's love in meaningful ways, especially as you speak words of approval.

STORIES FROM A HUSBAND'S HEART

My wife has set the standard in our family. She's led the way in sharing words of approval. She never puts me down, criticizes me, or picks over my faults. Instead, she makes it a point to approve of me in deeds and in words. And that has proved to be contagious. The more she honors me by showing her approval, the more I've wanted to do the same for her.

Here's what showing approval might look like:

- Displaying photos of your spouse on your desk or in your home. Taking photos or videos of your spouse's important life events. Wanting your friends or coworkers to meet your spouse.

- Here's what giving words of approval might sound like:
  - "I'm so proud to be your husband. I am so thankful that God brought us together."

- ° "I'm proud of you. It is such a blessing to be married to such a wise, sensitive woman."
- ° "I am so glad to be married to your daughter. She is God's precious gift for me" (said to wife's parents).

PRAY: LISTEN TO JESUS

I love you for who you are apart from what you do. You don't have to do anything to earn my love. My love for you is unconditional. I know everything there is to know about you, your strengths, and your weaknesses, and still, it was the possibility of a relationship with you that brought me to Calvary. You are my beloved, you are chosen. I am pleased with you, and you are one in whom I delight. (See Matthew 3:17; Exodus 33:17; Ephesians 1:7; 1 John 3:1).

* Jesus, when I reflect on how you love me apart from what I do, I feel grateful because _____. In considering that you endured Calvary because a relationship with me was important to you, I am moved with feelings of

   _____.

* Lord, I pray that my wife would sense this same approval from you. Give her a fresh experience of affirming love. Reassure her that you love her apart from what she does.

LIVE: DO THE BIBLE

Commend those who do right.

—1 Peter 2:14 NIV

* God, show me some of the ways I can give words of approval and commendation to my wife. What character traits should I affirm in her? Show me what you see in her. I want her to sense my pride because _____.

* God, I pray that my wife would see more and more opportunities to affirm, approve, and commend others. Reveal to her the positive aspects of thecharacter of others and empower her to verbalize them.

TAKE ACTION

● Do an internet search for a list of positive character traits. Choose two traits that are true about your wife each week. Share them with her verbally or in writing: "I am proud you are my wife because you are _____. I see that trait in you when _____."

● Post your wife's photo in your office. Brag on her often in front of your coworkers.

CLAIM HIS PROMISES

"Give, and it will be given to you."

—LUKE 6:38 NASB

Love People P-3:
A Spirit-empowered disciple loves people by discerning relational needs of others and sharing God's love in meaningful ways.

Day 19

CLOSENESS THROUGH TOUCH

Discern the relational needs of others and share God's love in meaningful ways, especially as you give them affection.

STORIES FROM A HUSBAND'S HEART

I have learned to love my wife in the way she longs to be loved. We have discovered that as I initiate affection without any strings attached, her fears decrease. Each time I hold her hand or rub her back, I am reassuring her of my love. She doesn't have to wonder, *Does he still love me?* My initiative to give to my wife in these tender ways deepens her trust in our relationship.

One of the practical ways we've practiced the art of affection is through our goodbyes and greetings. As we leave each other in the morning, my wife and I make sure to start the day with a hug. We'll give each other a hug and usually include a group hug with the kids. Greeting one another with a kiss at the end of a long day has also paid big benefits. It has taken concerted effort to stop what I'm doing or shake off the kid clinging to my leg. But with each greeting, my wife and I reestablish our commitment to one another.

PRAY: LISTEN TO JESUS

My love for you is an everlasting love; I want you to experience how wide, long, high, and deep my love is for you. Imagine it's evening and you are sitting safely on a boat in the middle of the ocean. The sea is perfectly calm, and the stars are shining brightly. My love is like the horizon. It doesn't end; you just can't see it all at once. My love is higher than the stars; you'll never be able to reach its limits. My love goes on forever; there are no time constraints or expiration dates. My love is deeper than the ocean floor; you'll never reach its end. I love you with an everlasting love. (See Isaiah 42:6; Jeremiah 31:3; 1 John 3:1; Ephesians 3:18.)

* Jesus, when I imagine that your care for me never ends, my heart is moved with gratitude because _____. When I reflect on your limitless and everlasting love, I am in awe of you because _____.

* Lord, I pray that my wife would sense the vastness of your love for her. I ask that you would overwhelm her in a new way with the height, the depth, and the extent of your love, especially as she _____.

LIVE: DO THE BIBLE

Greet one another with a holy kiss.

—ROMANS 16:16 NASB

* God, I want to communicate affection and closeness to my wife through my tender words and gentle touch. Help me know the right words to say because _____.

Help me know the right time and the meaningful ways to communicate my love for her, especially as _____.

* Lord, I pray that you would empower my wife to share her love through tender words and gentle touch. Help her share more and more of your love through _____.

TAKE ACTION

* Surprise your wife by going out of your way to creatively communicate that you love her. Write a love note that says, *I was thinking of you* _____, or *You are important to me because* _____.

* Make a sixty-second phone call during the day and say, "Hi, Sweetheart. I was just calling to say I love you. See you tonight. Bye."

* Leave your wife in the morning with a tender hug and kiss. Greet her when you arrive home with this same demonstration of closeness.

CLAIM HIS PROMISES

No one has seen God, ever. But if we love one another, God dwells deeply within us, and his love becomes complete in us—perfect love!

—1 JOHN 4:12 MSG

Love People P-3:
A Spirit-empowered disciple loves people by discerning relational needs of others and sharing God's love in meaningful ways.

Day 20

GRATITUDE AND APPRECIATION

Discern the relational needs of others and share God's love in meaningful ways, especially as you appreciate them.

STORIES FROM A HUSBAND'S HEART

When I come home from a long day at work, I am often preoccupied with my own concerns and may overlook what my wife has done that day. She has worked, volunteered, and kept our family running smoothly for over twenty years. There are days, however, when I hardly notice. I take it for granted that my laundry magically appears in the closet. I barely notice that the kitchen is always clean and the bills are paid on time. There are days when I don't even give a cursory thanks for the coffee that's made or that the kids get to school. There have been times when I've missed the hurt and disappointment in her eyes when I failed to express my appreciation.

The alternative can be extremely powerful. On the days when I let my wife know that I not only notice but greatly appreciate all she has done, her spirits lift, her step quickens, and her smile returns.

It only takes a few moments to express my gratitude: "Sweetheart, thank you so much for picking up the dry cleaning. Your time is valuable, and I appreciate your help." It only costs two minutes of time to send her a note that says, *Thank you for taking the kids to the zoo and giving me a few hours of quiet time.*

God has definitely given me a woman who is worthy to be praised. I need to be reminded to rise up and call her blessed.

PRAY: LISTEN TO JESUS

I am a God who sees. I see all your steps, I see all that you do and the effort you make, and I intercede on your behalf. You can count on me and my great name; I won't leave you or abandon you in the midst of all you do. (See Genesis 16:13; Job 34:21; Romans 8:27.)

* Jesus, it makes me feel so grateful to know that you are a God who sees because _____. I am thankful that you notice the things I do and that you intercede for me because _____. I'm grateful I can count on you to be with me in the midst of _____.

* Jesus, would you let my wife know that you see how she _____. Reassure her that you know and acknowledge her _____, even when I miss it.

LIVE: DO THE BIBLE

Her children arise and call her blessed;
her husband also, and he praises her.

—PROVERBS 31:28 NIV

* God, would you show me the things my wife does that may go unnoticed or that I take for granted? Empower me to rise up, take initiative, and tell her and the world about how much she does for me and for our family. I'm especially grateful today for how she _____.

* Lord, would you give my wife the special vision to see the things that others do and the effort they make? Empower her to speak up and say thank you often.

TAKE ACTION

* Appreciate your wife in front of the kids: "Kids, I want you to know that you have a very special mom. She is amazing and does so much for our family like _____."

* Bring home a special gift, a thoughtfully composed letter, or flowers as a demonstration of your appreciation.

* Share these words with your wife: "I'm so grateful for you and how you _____."

CLAIM HIS PROMISES

The Lord remembers us and will bless us.

—PSALM 115:12 HCSB

Love People P-3:

A Spirit-empowered disciple loves people by discerning relational needs of others and sharing God's love in meaningful ways.

Day 21

ENTERING ANOTHER'S WORLD

Discern the relational needs of others and share God's love in meaningful ways, especially as you give them attention.

STORIES FROM A HUSBAND'S HEART

Giving attention in marriage is sometimes difficult. It often means leaving my familiar, comfortable world and entering the uncomfortable world of my wife. It's helped me to remember that Jesus did the same for me. He left the comfort of heaven and entered this chaotic, sin-filled world.

To give attention means doing things with my wife that she enjoys doing. Giving attention means listening without interrupting so I can understand her and her world. It means asking about my her day and really wanting to hear the response. It means buying her favorite coffee or remembering her favorite flower. Attention also means spending time with her and giving her a focused, purposeful response. All of these send the message that I know and remember her world, and I'm blessed to share it with her.

I've discovered that as I leave my world and enter hers, we enjoy a deepened sense of oneness. Our friendship grows and there is an increased fondness in her eyes that is worth the world to me.

PRAY: LISTEN TO JESUS

I have set my love upon you. I will set you on high because I know your name. You will call upon me, and I will hear you. I will be with you in trouble; I will deliver you and honor you. Remember, I lean in to listen to the needs of your heart. The thoughts I have about you are precious, rare, and beautiful. I think about you so often, you couldn't even begin to count the times; they outnumber the sand of the seas. (See Psalm 4:3, 91:14–15, 139:17–18.)

* Jesus, it amazes me that you lean in and listen to me. I'm calling upon you today and trusting that you will hear me about _____. You are attentive to me and my world, and I give you thanks because _____.

* Lord, I pray that my wife would come to a new understanding of how attentive you are to her needs. Would you reassure her that you listen to her? Remind her of your attentiveness and thoughtfulness even when I miss the mark.

LIVE: DO THE BIBLE

That the members may have the same care for one another.

—1 CORINTHIANS 12:25 NASB

* God, show me how to care for my wife and give her attention. In what ways do I need to listen to her more effectively and understand her more deeply? What things can we enjoy doing that are part of her world?

* Lord, I pray that my wife would enjoy your attentiveness and then be more free to give to others. Reveal new ways that she can listen, understand, and enjoy giving to others as she enters their world.

TAKE ACTION

* Say this to your wife and be prepared to listen: "Hey, honey, tell me about your day."

* Watch a movie, try a hobby, or go to an event that purely appeals to your wife's interests.

* Say some of these sentences and be ready to follow through: "Let's do what you want to do tonight," or "I'd like to hear about some of your dreams and goals."

CLAIM HIS PROMISES

You faithfully answer our prayers with awesome deeds,
O God our savior.

—PSALM 65:5

Love People P-3:

A Spirit-empowered disciple loves people by discerning relational needs of others and sharing God's love in meaningful ways.

HONOR AND VALUE

Discern the relational needs of others and share God's love in meaningful ways, especially as you show them respect.

STORIES FROM A HUSBAND'S HEART

I am convinced that when you put toilet paper on the holder, you should do it so that the sheets come over the top rather than from below. I'm convinced there is a certain way to load the dishwasher to achieve maximum efficiency. I am convinced that it is much better to get somewhere early than to get there just on time.

While I am certain of all these things, they are my preferences. However, they are not necessarily my wife's. It's been a difficult journey, but I have learned that respect means regarding her needs and preferences just as highly as I do my own. It means I must consider that what is important to me may or may not be of value and importance to her. Also, even though it's important to me, it may not be all that important in light of eternity. Respect in a marriage means I may have to give up some of my preferences.

In our marriage, that means I may have to choose what is most important. Do I want my wife to show me respect by leaving for the airport in plenty of time, or could I choose to respect that she has many details to attend to before we leave for a trip? Do I need her to show me respect by loading the dishwasher a certain way, or could I choose to respect her need to feel appreciated and just be grateful it's all getting done?

PRAY: LISTEN TO JESUS

I place great value on our relationship; in fact, I call you my friend. I chose you and appointed you, that you should go and bear fruit and bring honor to my name. Remember that when you call on me, I will rescue you and honor you because I love you. Before honor comes humility, so make sure that you see others as more important than yourself. Give honor to all people. (See John 15:15–16; Psalm 91:15; Proverbs 18:12; Philippians 2:3, 1 Peter 2:17).

* Jesus, I feel respected that you would call me your friend because _____. When I imagine that you have chosen and appointed me, I feel grateful for this honor because _____.

* Lord, I pray that you would remind my wife that you have chosen her. You have appointed her to be your friend. This is a divine honor. Help her embrace and experience all that this means for her, especially as she _____.

LIVE: DO THE BIBLE

Be devoted to one another in love. Honor one another above yourselves.

—ROMANS 12:10 NIV

* God, please show me new ways I can honor and respect my wife. In what ways can I defer to her and let go of my preferences? Show me topics that need her input, ideas, and feedback. In what ways do I need to think more highly of her than I do myself? I know she needs my respect in these areas: _____.

* Lord, I pray that you would empower my wife to give honor to _____. Help her show respect in this area: _____. Enable her to think more highly of _____ in this way: _____.

TAKE ACTION

• Ask your wife, "You're so good at helping me think through things. What do you think I should do about _____?" or "Your opinion is really important to me, so what's your opinion about _____?"

• Arrive on time for events that are important to your wife. Keep spending within the family budget and honor financial agreements. Listen to her perspective and ask for her ideas.

CLAIM HIS PROMISES

The wise are promoted to honor, but fools are promoted to shame!

—PROVERBS 3:35 TLB

Love People P-3:

A Spirit-empowered disciple loves people by discerning relational needs of others and sharing God's love in meaningful ways.

Day 23

BEARING THE LOAD

Discern the relational needs of others and share God's love in meaningful ways, especially as you support them.

STORIES FROM A HUSBAND'S HEART

It took me a while, but I finally realized that God didn't intend for some of us to be the ones always giving support, while other people were exclusively receiving support. We have the opportunity to bear the burdens of those around us, but we also have the privilege of allowing others to bear our burdens. That's sometimes hard for a tough guy like me.

What this has meant in our marriage is that there are times when I need to be vulnerable with my needs. I have to be willing to admit my weaknesses, struggles, and need for help. It may seem like a no-brainer, but I've had to work hard at saying things like, "Honey, I'm feeling really overwhelmed with work right now. Would you have some time to help me this weekend?"

I've also learned the importance and payoff of inviting my wife to be vulnerable with her need for support. One of the most loving things I can say to her is, "Sweetheart, I know you have a lot on your plate. Is there anything I can do to help?" That sentence alone can change the entire climate of our home.

PRAY: LISTEN TO JESUS

I will accomplish what concerns you. My lovingkindness is everlasting, so I will not forsake the works of my hands. I will equip you with everything good—that you may be able to do the things I have called you to do, the work which is pleasing in my sight. As you receive my care and support, be sure to offer the same to others. When you carry their burdens, you're living out my commands. (See Psalm 138:8; Hebrews 13:20–21; Galatians 6:2.)

* Jesus, when I read your words and know that you will accomplish what concerns me, I am thankful because _____. To know that you have equipped me with everything I need to do the work you've called me to do, makes me incredibly grateful because _____.

* Lord, remind my wife that she has been equipped by the living God for _____. You have promised to accomplish _____. You have called her to _____, and you will not forsake the work of your hands.

LIVE: DO THE BIBLE

Carry each other's burdens, and in this way you will fulfill the law of Christ.

—GALATIANS 6:2 NIV

* God, show me ways that I can help share in my wife's burdens. How can I help relieve the burden of her to-do list, emotions that are heavy, or concerns of the heart? Show me practical ways I can pitch in and bring relief.

* Lord, empower my wife to receive support from you and then look for ways to give to others. Help her see opportunities to bear other people's burdens and fulfill your command.

TAKE ACTION

* Take initiative to help out with household chores that are typically your wife's responsibility. Ask, "Is there anything else I can do to shorten your list?"

* Say to your wife, "I'm committed to work alongside you and get this done" and "Could we take a few minutes and pray together about this?"

CLAIM HIS PROMISES

It is more blessed to give than to receive.

—ACTS 20:35

Love People P-3: A Spirit-empowered disciple loves people by discerning relational needs of others and sharing God's love in meaningful ways.

Day 24

SAFE AND SECURE

Discern the relational needs of others and share God's love in meaningful ways, especially as you reassure them and bring security to your relationship.

STORIES FROM A HUSBAND'S HEART

As you receive security from God, you can give security in marriage. To give security means you live in such a way that you let your wife know that you are committed to her and her only, that you will always be true to your wedding vows and forsake all others.

Security means providing for the financial needs of your family. It may mean operating on a budget, having a good work ethic, developing marketable skills, or providing a secure financial future in case of illness or death.

Security means refraining from making threats to leave or abandon your family. It means committing to protecting your family from physical and emotional harm, including refraining from harming your wife or children in any way. It is not losing your temper or raising your voice and being dependable by keeping promises.

An intimate marriage is only possible when both spouses feel confident in a reassuring, safe, and caring relationship. An intimate family is only possible when all members feel secure.

PRAY: LISTEN TO JESUS

I promise to never leave you or forsake you. I will always meet your needs. I will be your ever-present help in times of trouble. You can count on me to be faithful, unchangeable, and constant. I give security for those who trust in me as their Savior. The mountains may be removed and the hills may shake, but my lovingkindness will not be removed. My promise of peace will not be shaken. I will set you securely on high and protect you fiercely because you have known my name. (See Psalm 46:1, 91:14-15; Lamentations 3:23; Hebrews 13:8; John 10:28; Isaiah 54:10.)

* Jesus, I'm grateful for your reassurance about _____. I'm thankful for how you have given me security that _____. I am counting on you to _____.

* Lord, give my wife an extra dose of your security and protection. Reassure her that _____. Remind her that you are her ever-present help, fierce protector, and unchangeable stability when _____.

LIVE: DO THE BIBLE

God has not given us a spirit of fear.

—2 TIMOTHY 1:7 NIV

* God, I want to be a source of your security for my wife. In what ways can I give her reassurance, protection, and stability? What does she need most from me at this time? Speak, Lord. I want to hear from you.

* Lord, I pray that you would empower my wife to be a source of your security as well. Show her opportunities to give reassurance, protection, and stability to others.

TAKE ACTION

• Say these things to your wife: "I love you and I'll always love you, no matter what," "If I had to do it all over again, you're the one I would choose to spend my life with," and "I'm committed to you and to our marriage."

• Meet your wife's financial needs by living within the agreed-upon budget through careful planning.

• Meet her relational security needs by never referencing divorce or separation, or comparing her to other women.

CLAIM HIS PROMISES

"Love each other. Just as I have loved you, you should love each other."

—JOHN 13:34

Love People P-3:
A Spirit-empowered disciple loves people by discerning relational needs of others and sharing God's love in meaningful ways.

Notes

Notes

Notes

A SPIRIT-EMPOWERED DISCIPLE

Lives His Mission

Day 25

RECEIVE IT
THEN SHARE IT

Actively share your life with others and tell them about the Jesus who lives in you as you live a grace-filled life in front of them.

STORIES FROM A HUSBAND'S HEART

Grace can't be earned or deserved. It is a gift freely given by the Giver who has an endless supply. Receiving grace from God makes giving grace to others possible. In fact, God calls me to give from His boundless supply.

It's only as I experience and receive more of God's grace, that I have something to give to others. If I struggle with forgiving my wife, I might first need to explore the forgiveness that God gives. If I struggle to accept her, I might need a fresh experience of God's unconditional acceptance for me.

As a recipient of God's unlimited grace, I experience gratitude that empowers my giving. For instance, I remember the absolute disbelief and gratitude I felt when I realized that God—in spite of all I had done, and in spite of my open rebellion to any kind of authority, including His—could love me and save me from eternal separation from Him. When I consider God's grace for me, I can do nothing less than pass that same kind of grace along to others.

This principle of first receiving God's grace and then giving it has allowed my wife and me to share a powerful story of hope with other couples. We've been able to say, "When I ran out of acceptance, I turned to the God who loves me unconditionally" and "When we struggle to forgive each other, we go to the God whose lovingkindness is everlasting." Gratitude for His grace in our marriage has empowered our testimony of hope that we share with others.

PRAY: LISTEN TO JESUS

I couldn't bear the thought of heaven without you, so I gave you the ultimate gift. Remember, my gift of grace is new every morning; it never runs out. I'm available every moment to help you carry life's burdens and meet its challenges. Experience and receive my grace, honor me with your thanks, and then share my grace with others. (See Lamentations 3:23; Psalm 50:23, 68:19; 1 Peter 4:10.)

* Jesus, I am grateful your grace is new every morning because I need more of your _____ today. Would you infuse me with a fresh dose of your _____ for _____ my wife?

* Lord, I pray that my wife would experience a new gift of your _____. Would you infuse her with a fresh dose of your _____ for me?

LIVE: DO THE BIBLE

As each one has received a special gift, employ it in serving one another as good stewards of the manifold grace of God.

—1 PETER 4:10 NASB

* God, I have received your gift of _____, and now I want to give it to my wife. I also want to share the hope that is in me with someone else. Who needs to hear about your grace and how it has empowered me to give?

* Lord, I pray that you would show my wife who might need to hear her story of God's grace and how it has empowered her to give.

TAKE ACTION

* Talk to your wife about the ways you have both received God's grace and how it has empowered your giving to one another. Pray together about who might need to hear your story.

CLAIM HIS PROMISES

I can do all things through him who strengthens me.

—PHILIPPIANS 4:13 ESV

Live His Mission M-1:

A Spirit-empowered disciple lives His mission by actively sharing his life with others and telling them about the Jesus who lives inside of him.

Day 26

THE ZACCHAEUS PRINCIPLE

Actively share your life with others and tell them about the Jesus who lives in you, specifically as He empowers you to look beyond faults and see needs.

STORIES FROM A HUSBAND'S HEART

Zacchaeus—a hated tax collector, a traitor to his own people, and a thief—was no doubt often ridiculed and attacked for his sins. Lonely and curious, he climbed a tree to get a good look at the Messiah. He had to wonder if Jesus would notice him. And if He did, would He also reject him? (See Luke 19:1–27.)

What a miracle Christ's call must have been to this outcast! Our Savior asked Zacchaeus to share a meal, inviting him into one of the most intimate social settings of the day. This simple invitation from Jesus was a deliberate offer of welcome, reception, and loving relationship. Jesus looked beyond the faults of Zacchaeus and saw his need.

In the midst of Zacchaeus' failures, Jesus offered compassion, companionship, and acceptance. It's interesting to note what Jesus didn't do that day: He didn't attack the tax collector's behavior, point out things that were wrong with him, or even give helpful advice. He didn't remind Zacchaeus of what he should be doing or criticize him for not taking more responsibility. Jesus didn't quote Scripture or make comparisons with other tax collectors in town. He didn't try to manipulate change in Zacchaeus or withhold affection from him.

My wife and I have experienced the blessing of the Zacchaeus Principle—to look beyond our partner's faults and see his or her needs. It doesn't go well for us to attack each other, point out things that are wrong, criticize, compare, manipulate, or withhold. Instead, we ask God for a fresh reminder of how He has looked beyond *our* faults and then ask for His help to do the same for others.

PRAY: LISTEN TO JESUS

I came to seek and to save you! I didn't wait until you shaped up or acted right. I looked beyond your faults and loved you while you were still a sinner. The world needs my kind of love; there's too much comparison, criticism, and selfishness. Look for opportunities to share how my love for you has changed your relationship with your wife. (See Luke 19:1–27; Romans 5:8.)

* Jesus, when I reflect on how you have looked past my faults and met my needs, I am filled with gratitude because _____. God, would you remind me of the awesome deeds you have done in my life and marriage, particularly in how you have allowed me to look beyond faults and see needs?

* Lord, I pray that you would give my wife a fresh experience of gratitude for how you have changed our relationship. Give her insight into how you have empowered us to look beyond one another's faults to see and meet needs.

LIVE: DO THE BIBLE

Come and see the works of God,
who is awesome in His deeds
toward the sons of men.

—PSALM 66:5 NASB

* God, as I have come to have your same perspective with my wife and our marriage, I'm grateful you have changed me and our relationship by _____. I'm thankful because _____. Who needs to hear and see your works? Give me opportunities to share your deeds.

* Lord, I pray you would remind my wife of what you have done in her and in our marriage. Give her opportunities to tell others about your deeds.

TAKE ACTION

* Talk with your wife about how the Zacchaeus Principle has been true for you. Look for opportunities to share your story with others.

CLAIM HIS PROMISES

I pray that the sharing of your faith may become effective for the full knowledge of every good thing that is in us for the sake of Christ.

—PHILEMON 1:6 ESV

Live His Mission M-1:

A Spirit-empowered disciple lives His mission by actively sharing his life with others and telling them about the Jesus who lives inside of him.

Day 27

VULNERABILITY

Actively share your life with others and tell them about the Jesus who lives in you, especially as you are vulnerable with your weaknesses and struggles.

STORIES FROM A HUSBAND'S HEART

Marital trust is such a delicate thing. It can be lost gradually by many small wrongs or instantly by one huge wrong. Living in a fallen world and being married to an imperfect person makes us vulnerable. It also challenges us to trust God and then our spouse.

Given that everyone is imperfect, building trust within marriage is critical for a lifelong relationship. Trust is the glue that binds relationships together in times of failure and struggle.

To build trust, start by totally putting your confidence in God because He is the only One righteous and worthy of your faith. You are called to trust God with your wife, knowing that since everyone is human, she will to some degree fail to meet your expectations. It is these occasions that provide the most important fork in the road. When you don't know what to do, your eyes must be on God (2 Chronicles 20:12). When your wife fails, turn to God for help, and He will be your ultimate security.

In an age of cynicism and skepticism, a faith-filled marriage is a powerful ambassador for Christ, as it calls attention to the health of the relationship and the One who is making it healthy. The testimony of our deepened trust speaks loudly about the One who is at work to knit our hearts together.

PRAY: LISTEN TO JESUS

You can put your trust in me. I am faithful and I am trustworthy in all I do. I am so trustworthy that I am surrounded by faithfulness. When you don't know what to do or you don't know where to turn, come to me. Let your focus be on me. As we walk together through the struggles of this world, we'll show others what it looks like to be my disciple. When you love one another even when it's hard, people will become convinced that I am the source of love. (See 2 Corinthians 1:18–20; Psalm 33:4; 89:8; 1 Peter 3:15.)

* Jesus, I am grateful that I can trust you to _____. I don't know what to do about _____, so my eyes are on you.

* Lord, remind my wife that you are faithful and she can trust you to _____. Please give her a renewed focus on you, so he knows what to do about _____.

LIVE: DO THE BIBLE

If someone asks about your hope as a believer, always be ready to explain it.

—1 PETER 3:15

* God, I want to share about my hope and trust in you. Empower me to be vulnerable about my struggle with _____ and how I am trusting you to _____. I have hope in you about _____, so give me the words and the opportunity to share this hope with those who don't yet know you.

* Lord, would you give my wife the opportunities to share her story of hope with others? She is trusting you to _____, so give her the words to share with those who don't yet know you.

TAKE ACTION

• Talk with your wife about the struggles you have had in the past and how your trust in God brought healing, resolution or peace. Pray together, asking for opportunities to share your testimony of hope with others.

CLAIM HIS PROMISES

Depend on God and keep at it because in the Lord God you have a sure thing.

—ISAIAH 26:4 MSG

Live His Mission M-1:

A Spirit-empowered disciple lives His mission by actively sharing his life with others and telling them about the Jesus who lives inside of him.

Day 28

ONE OF A KIND

Actively share your life with others and tell them about the Jesus who lives in you, specifically as you seize opportunities that arise in your daily life.

STORIES FROM A HUSBAND'S HEART

There isn't a sport that I don't like to watch or play—any game, any time. I love the action and the adrenaline. God has blessed me with a passion for sports and an ability to coach and play a few of them.

My wife is the opposite. In fact, she couldn't care less about sports. She'd much rather be repainting, retiling, or re-stenciling something. She is a decorating genius.

Here's the amazing thing we've discovered about our vastly different interests. My interest in sports and her passion for decorating have allowed us to develop special friendships with people who need Jesus. What once was an area of conflict between us is now an opportunity to reach people for Christ. Some weekends, my wife goes to other people's homes to help them redo a bathroom or repaint a bedroom. By the time she leaves, she's developed enough of a friendship that she invites them to our house to watch the next NFL or NBA game. When game time comes, we invite that couple, plus a few Jesus-followers, to our home and continue the relationship. It's been amazing. We're seeing friends come to Christ *because* of our different interests and passions!

PRAY: LISTEN TO JESUS

I've formed you with unique talents, interests, and abilities. I created you with these gifts so that you can be a one-of-a-kind expression of me. I placed all these abilities in you so that you can do the great things I have planned—like introduce others to me. I love to see you live out your interests and enjoy life, and I love seeing you bring my hope to this world. (See Colossians 1:27).

* Jesus, when I imagine that you created me to be a one-of-a-kind expression of you and that you gave me these gifts to draw others to you, I feel _____.

* Lord, remind my wife of how she is a one-of-a-kind expression of you and how she is uniquely called to draw others to you with her gifts. Give her a renewed sense of your calling as she _____.

LIVE: DO THE BIBLE

Let us not love in word or talk but in deed and in truth.

—1 JOHN 3:18 ESV

* God, show me the ways you would like me to share your love in practical ways. How can I use the opportunities, gifts, and talents you have given me on a daily basis to

create spiritual conversations about you? Speak to me, Lord. I am listening.

* God, I pray you would show my wife the unique opportunities you give her every day to love others and point them to you.

TAKE ACTION

• Talk and pray with your wife about how the two of you might work together to combine your daily interests, passions, and lifestyle to cultivate friends who are not yet followers of Jesus. Make plans for building these friendships and sharing the love of Jesus.

CLAIM HIS PROMISES

I am not ashamed of the gospel, for it is the power of God for salvation to everyone who believes.

—ROMANS 1:16 ESV

Live His Mission M-1:

A Spirit-empowered disciple lives His mission by actively sharing his life with others and telling them about the Jesus who lives inside of him.

Day 29

EVERYDAY BLESSINGS

Actively share your life with others and tell them about the Jesus who lives in you.

STORIES FROM A HUSBAND'S HEART

The times when God has surprised me with His loving care have been some of my greatest reasons for praise.

For example, I remember the time I lost a fifty-dollar bill in an airport. I was terribly distraught over losing what was to me a large sum of money. But the following week, in a completely different location, I found a fifty-dollar bill literally lying at my feet. There was absolutely no one around to claim it or anyplace to turn it in. Even though I had never asked the Lord to replace the money I had lost, I know God put that money there just to remind me of His watchful care.

Another example of this surprising care is the time when my wife and I took a trip to Africa, where we had the privilege of touring on a safari. I had always been fascinated with animals, so this particular trip was sheer pleasure for me. We saw animals that even the National Geographic photographer had not seen in his twelve years of experience. I never thought to ask the Lord for His abundant provision on the safari. I think He just wanted to show me how much He cared for me. I was incredibly grateful.

It feels good when someone cares enough to know what makes you happy and does it without being asked. Those can be some of the more blessed moments in marriage.

PRAY: LISTEN TO JESUS

Look for people who might need you to share your life and the gospel. Begin by taking time to be with me. One of the identifying features of my disciples is that they love to be with me. Next, be sure to share your life and the gospel with your wife, children, and family. Then you'll want to share the good news with neighbors, coworkers, and people of your community. Share not only the salvation story, but also the everyday blessings I bring to your life. (See Matthew 28:19–20.)

* Jesus, make me more aware of the everyday blessings you bring to my life and give me opportunities to tell others about those blessings. I want to brag on you about _____.

* Lord, please make my wife more aware of the everyday blessings you bring to her life. Give her opportunities to tell others about those blessings. Empower her to _____.

LIVE: DO THE BIBLE

We loved you so much that we shared with you not only God's Good News but our own lives, too.
—1 Thessalonians 2:8

* God, show me who needs to hear your Good News and the ways you have blessed my life. Speak to me, Lord. I am listening. Give me opportunities and empowerment.

* Lord, please show my wife the people who need to hear about your Good News and the ways you have blessed her life. Give her opportunities and empowerment.

TAKE ACTION

* First, talk with your wife about the ways that God has made a difference in your marriage, then look for opportunities to tell your Jesus story to another person or couple. Share how Jesus is changing you, your life, and your marriage.

* Look for ways to connect with unchurched couples. Invite them to your home, do life together, and share the hope that is within you.

CLAIM HIS PROMISES

Everything is from God, who reconciled us to himself through Christ and gave us the ministry of reconciliation.

—2 CORINTHIANS 5:18 HCSB

Live His Mission M-1:

A Spirit-empowered disciple lives His mission by actively sharing his life with others and telling them about the Jesus who lives inside of him.

Day 30

MOVE TOWARD
THE DIFFERENCES

Actively share your life with others and tell them about the Jesus who lives in you, especially as you celebrate how you and your wife are more alike than different.

STORIES FROM A HUSBAND'S HEART

My wife's counseling practice was booming. It was tough for her to take a restroom break, much less go out for lunch. I became worried about my wife missing lunch every day. After all, food is an absolute priority for me!

I was so concerned about this that I bought her a small refrigerator for her office. I even went out of my way to keep it stocked. I was very proud of myself for thinking of my wife and caring for her in such an important way. But my pride turned to frustration when I realized that she often got too busy with paperwork and forgot the food that I had lovingly provided.

I was about to rip the refrigerator out of the office when the Lord impressed me with these thoughts: *I know it's frustrating because your wife has different ways of doing things. That's got to be okay. She may need a relational reason to stop and eat lunch just like you need relational motivation to go to the gym.*

I kept stocking that refrigerator, but I also tried something new. I'd call my wife once a week and ask to meet her at *her office* for lunch. This touch of personal involvement gave her a feeling of being truly cared for, and we enjoyed some great lunches together. I came to understand that she appreciated my efforts, but that she just handles things differently. What made her stop and receive support was our common connection and enjoyment of being together. We are so notably different that experiences like these have enabled us to share with others that it is God who brings us together.

PRAY: LISTEN TO JESUS

You are my workmanship. Remember though, your wife is also my beautiful creation. Both of you were lovingly crafted with unique gifts, talents, and personalities. I've designed special purposes for each of you; I've created special plans for you to accomplish together. Come to me and listen. I'll share them with you. Celebrate the special plans that I have ordained for you as a couple and then tell the world about the wonderful things we get to do together. (See Ephesians 2:10.)

* Jesus, remind me often of the special purposes you have designed for my wife. I celebrate the unique way she _____. We are certainly different in the way we _____, but what plans have you ordained for us together?

* Lord, reveal more of the special calling and purpose you have for my wife. Show her more of the plans you have ordained for us together.

LIVE: DO THE BIBLE

Tell of His glory among the nations,
His wonderful deeds among all the peoples.

—1 CHRONICLES 16:24 NASB

* God, as we come together in unity about the special plans you have for us, empower us to tell the world about your wonderful works. Give us opportunities to tell more people about the deeds you have done in our marriage.

* Lord, I pray you would bring unity and clarity of vision about how my wife and I share our faith with others. Let our unity be a confirmation of your plans and purposes.

TAKE ACTION

• Talk and pray with your wife about the celebrations of what the Lord has done in your marriage and how He has brought a beautiful story out of your differences.

• Pray together about how and where the Lord might want you share your celebrations with others.

CLAIM HIS PROMISES

A spiritual gift is given to each of us so we can help each other.

—1 CORINTHIANS 12:7

Live His Mission M-1:
A Spirit-empowered disciple lives His mission by actively sharing his life with others and telling them about the Jesus who lives inside of him.

Day 31

KINDNESS
IS POWERFUL

Actively share your life with others and tell them about the Jesus who lives in you; specifically, share the gospel's power of kindness.

STORIES FROM A HUSBAND'S HEART

My wife and I have discovered that it's usually difficult for couples to discuss areas of needed growth in their marriage. Too often, they are detoured by defensiveness, blame, and complaint.

We counseled a couple to help them learn a few tips about how to share their desires for change with kindness. First, we asked them to prepare a list of thanks: a list of things they were thankful for in their marriage and in one another. After completing their respective lists, they were to share them out loud with each other. This discussion helped reassure both of them that they were pleased with specific aspects of their marriage, and they were able to see good things in each other.

Next, we asked them to prepare a list of wishes: a list that included specific, positive statements about what they might like to see different in their marriage. The husband included this statement: *I'm hoping you might become more comfortable initiating affection.* The wife stated this wish: *I wish we could be more consistent about having family dinner.*

The couple shared their entire list of wishes, being careful to communicate with kindness and respect. This helped them avoid the destructive cycle of having expectations they didn't share, then becoming hurt and angry when expectations weren't met. Communicating their wishes with kindness helped them express specific needs, not just negative generalities. It also helped them avoid saying hurtful, negative words. As a final result, the kinder, gentler approach produced the desired change in their relationship and gave them fresh stories of God's work to share with others.

PRAY: LISTEN TO JESUS

It will be my heart of love, expressed through my people, that will draw a searching world to ask about me. Spend time meditating on my kindness toward you, then demonstrate that kindness with your wife. It's great practice for sharing my kindness with others! When people who don't know me receive some of my acceptance, encouragement, comfort, and support delivered through you, they will begin to wonder where you got all that kindness. At that point, you'll be ready to ready to talk about the hope that is inside you. It's their experience of kindness that opens the door for the gospel. (See 1 Peter 3:15; Romans 2:4, 15:7; Galatians 6:2; 2 Corinthians 1:3–4.)

* Jesus, I'm overwhelmed by your kindness toward me, specifically how you _____.

* Lord, reveal more of your kindness to my wife. Remind her of your _____.

LIVE: DO THE BIBLE

Or do you think lightly of the riches of His kindness and tolerance and patience, not knowing that the kindness of God leads you to repentance?

—ROMANS 2:4 NASB

* God, because of your kindness toward me, I want to give more of your _____ to my wife. I also want to give more of your _____ to others.

* Lord, overwhelm my wife with more of your kindness, as she gives more of your _____ to others.

TAKE ACTION

• Celebrate the powerful impact of kindness in your relationship. Talk and pray together about sharing your marriage story with others, giving testimony of the One who is the source of your joy.

CLAIM HIS PROMISES

You will be a witness for him to everyone of what you have seen and heard.

—ACTS 22:15 ESV

Live His Mission M-1:
A Spirit-empowered disciple lives His mission by actively sharing his life with others and telling them about the Jesus who lives inside him.

Notes

ABOUT THE
GREAT COMMANDMENT NETWORK

The Great Commandment Network is an international collaborative network of strategic kingdom leaders from the faith community, marketplace, education, and caregiving fields who prioritize the powerful simplicity of the words of Jesus to love God, love others, and see others become His followers (Matthew 22:37–40, Matthew 28:19–20).

THE GREAT COMMANDMENT NETWORK IS SERVED THROUGH THE FOLLOWING:

Relationship Press – This team collaborates, supports, and joins together with churches, denominational partners, and professional associates to develop, print, and produce resources that facilitate ongoing Great Commandment ministry.

The Center for Relational Leadership – Their mission is to teach, train, and mentor both ministry and corporate leaders in Great Commandment principles, seeking to equip leaders with relational skills so they might lead as Jesus led.

The Galatians 6:6 Retreat Ministry – This ministry offers a unique two-day retreat for ministers and their spouses for personal renewal and for reestablishing and affirming ministry and family priorities.

The Center for Relational Care (CRC) – The CRC provides therapy and support to relationships in crisis through an accelerated process of growth and healing, including Relational Care Intensives for couples, families, and singles.

A SPIRIT-EMPOWERED FAITH

Expresses Itself in Great Commission Living
Empowered by Great Commandment Love

**begins with the end in mind:
The Great Commission calls us
to make disciples.**

*"Go therefore and make disciples of all the nations, baptizing them in
the name of the Father and the Son and the Holy Spirit teaching them
to observe all things that I have commanded you; and lo, I am with
you always, even to the end of the age."* (Matthew 28:19–20)

The ultimate goal of our faith journey is to relate to the person of Jesus, because it is our relational connection to Jesus that will produce Christ-likeness and spiritual growth. This relational perspective of discipleship is required if we hope to have a faith that is marked by the Spirit's power.

Models of discipleship that are based solely upon what we *know* and what we *do* are incomplete, lacking the empowerment of a life of loving and living intimately with Jesus. **A Spirit-empowered faith is relational and impossible to realize apart from a special work of the Spirit.** For example, the Spirit-empowered outcome of "listening to and hearing God" implies relationship—it is both relational in focus and requires the Holy Spirit's power to live.

**begins at the right place:
The Great Commandment calls us to
start with loving God and loving others.**

*"'You shall love the Lord your God with all your heart, with all your soul,
and with all your mind.' This is the first and great commandment.
And the second is like it: 'You shall love your neighbor as yourself.'
On these two commandments hang all the Law and the Prophets."*

(Matthew 22:37–40)

Relevant discipleship does not begin with doctrines or teaching, parables or stewardship—but with loving the Lord with all your heart, mind, soul, and strength and then loving the people closest to you. Since Matthew 22:37–40 gives us the first and greatest commandment, *a Spirit-empowered faith starts where the Great Commandment tells us to start: A disciple must first learn to deeply love the Lord and to express His love to the "nearest ones"—his or her family, church, and community (and in that order).*

 embraces a relational process of Christlikeness.

Scripture reminds us that there are three sources of light for our journey: Jesus, His Word, and His people. The process of discipleship (or becoming more like Jesus) occurs as we relate intimately with each source of light.

"Walk while you have the light, lest darkness overtake you." (John 12:35)

Spirit-empowered discipleship will require a lifestyle of:
- Fresh encounters with Jesus (John 8:12)
- Frequent experiences of Scripture (Psalm 119:105)
- Faithful engagement with God's people (Matthew 5:14)

 can be defined with observable outcomes using a biblical framework.

The metrics for measuring Spirit-empowered faith or the growth of a disciple come from Scripture and are organized/framed around four distinct dimensions of a disciple who serves.

And He Himself gave some to be apostles, some prophets,
some evangelists, and some pastors and teachers,
for the equipping of the saints for the work of ministry,
for the edifying of the body of Christ.
(Ephesians 4:11–12)

A relational framework for organizing Spirit-Empowered Discipleship Outcomes draws from a cluster analysis of several Greek (*diakoneo, leitourgeo, douleuo*) and Hebrew words (*'abad, Sharat*), which elaborate on the Ephesians 4:12 declaration that Christ's followers are to be equipped for works of ministry or service. Therefore, the 40 Spirit-Empowered Faith Outcomes have been identified and organized around:

* Serving/loving the Lord – *While they were **ministering** to the Lord and fasting* (Acts 13:2 NASB).[1]
* Serving/loving the Word – *But we will devote ourselves to prayer and to the **ministry** of the word* (Acts 6:4 NASB).[2]
* Serving/loving people – *Through love **serve** one another* (Galatians 5:13 NASB).[3]
* Serving/loving His mission – *Now all these things are from God, who reconciled us to Himself through Christ and gave us the **ministry** of reconciliation* (2 Corinthians 5:18 NASB).[4]

1 Ferguson, David L. *Great Commandment Principle*. Cedar Park, Texas: Relationship Press, 2013.
2 Ferguson, David L. *Relational Foundations*. Cedar Park, Texas: Relationship Press, 2004.
3 Ferguson, David L. *Relational Discipleship*. Cedar Park, Texas: Relationship Press, 2005.
4 "Spirit Empowered Outcomes," www.empowered21.com, Empowered 21 Global Council, http://empowered21.com/discipleship-materials/.

A SPIRIT-EMPOWERED DISCIPLE LOVES THE LORD THROUGH

L1. Practicing thanksgiving in all things
Enter into His gates with thanksgiving (Ps. 100:4). *In everything give thanks* (1 Th. 5:18). *As sorrowful, yet always rejoicing* (2 Cor. 6:10).

L2. Listening to and hearing God for direction and discernment
"Speak, LORD, for Your servant hears" (1 Sam. 3:8–9). *Mary, who also sat at Jesus' feet and heard His word* (Lk. 10:38–42). *And the LORD said, "Shall I hide from Abraham what I am doing … ?"* (Gen. 18:17). *But as the same anointing teaches you concerning all things …* (1 Jn. 2:27).

L3. Experiencing God as He really is through deepened intimacy with Him
"Hear, O Israel: The LORD our God, the LORD is one! You shall love the LORD your God with all your heart, with all your soul, and with all your strength" (Deut. 6:4–5). *Therefore the LORD will wait, that He may be gracious to you; and therefore He will be exalted, that He may have mercy on you. For the LORD is a God of justice …* (Is. 30:18). See also John 14:9.

L4. Rejoicing regularly in my identity as "His Beloved"
And his banner over me was love (Song of Sol. 2:4). *To the praise of the glory of His grace, by which He made us accepted in the Beloved* (Eph. 1:6). *For so He gives His beloved sleep* (Ps. 127:2).

L5. Living with a passionate longing for purity and to please Him in all things
Who may ascend into the hill of the LORD? … He who has clean hands and a pure heart (Ps. 24:3–4). *Beloved, let us cleanse ourselves from all filthiness of flesh and spirit, perfecting holiness in the fear of God* (2 Cor. 7:1). *"I always do those things that please Him"* (Jn. 8:29). *"Though He slay me, yet will I trust Him"* (Job 13:15).

L6.   Consistent practice of self-denial, fasting, and solitude rest
He turned and said to Peter, "Get behind me, Satan! You are offense to Me, for you are not mindful of the things of God, but the things of men" (Mt. 16:23). "But you, when you fast …" (Mt. 6:17). "Be still, and know that I am God" (Ps. 46:10).

L7.   Entering often into Spirit-led praise and worship
Bless the LORD, O my soul, and all that is within me (Ps. 103:1). Serve the LORD with fear (Ps. 2:11). I thank You, Father, Lord of heaven and earth (Mt. 11:25).

L8.   Disciplined, bold, and believing prayer
Praying always with all prayer and supplication in the Spirit (Eph. 6:18). "Call to Me, and I will answer you" (Jer. 33:3). If we ask anything according to His will, He hears us. And if we know that He hears us, whatever we ask, we know that we have the petitions that we have asked of Him (1 Jn. 5:14–15).

L9.   Faithful stewardship and exercise of the gifts of the Spirit for empowered living and sacrifice
By one Spirit we were all baptized into one body—whether Jews or Greeks, whether slaves or free—and have all been made to drink into one Spirit (1 Cor. 12:13). "But you shall receive power when the Holy Spirit has come upon you" (Acts 1:8). But the manifestation of the Spirit is given to each one for the profit of all (1 Cor. 12:7). See also 1 Pet. 4:10 and Rom. 12:6.

L10.   Practicing the presence of the Lord, yielding to the Spirit's work of Christlikeness
But we all, with unveiled face, … are being transformed into the same from glory to glory, just as by the Spirit of the Lord (2 Cor. 3:18). As the deer pants for the water brooks, so pants my soul after You, O God (Ps. 42:1).

A SPIRIT-EMPOWERED DISCIPLE LIVES THE WORD THROUGH

W1. Frequently being led by the Spirit into deeper love for the One who wrote the Word

" 'You shall love the Lord your God … .' 'You shall love neighbor as yourself.' On these two commandments hang all the Law and the Prophets" (Mt. 22:37–40). And I will delight myself in Your commandments, which I love. (Ps. 119:47). "The fear of the Lord is clean … . More to be desired are they than gold … sweeter also than honey" (Ps. 19:9–10).

W2. Being a "living epistle" in reverence and awe as His Word becomes real in my life, vocation, and calling

You are our epistle written in our hearts, known and read by all men (2 Cor. 3:2). And the Word became flesh and dwelt among us (Jn. 1:14). Husbands, love your wives … cleanse her with the washing of water by the word (Eph. 5:25–26). See also Tit. 2:5. And whatever you do, do it heartily, as to the Lord and not to men (Col. 3:23).

W3. Yielding to the Scripture's protective cautions and transforming power to bring life change in me

Through Your precepts I get understanding; therefore I hate every false way (Ps. 119:104). "Let it be to me according to your word" (Lk. 1:38). How can a young man cleanse his way? By taking heed according to Your word (Ps. 119:9). See also Col. 3:16–17.

W4. Humbly and vulnerably sharing of the Spirit's transforming work through the Word

I will speak of your testimonies also before kings, and will not be ashamed (Ps. 119:46). Preach the word! Be ready in season and out of season (2 Tim. 4:2).

W5.   Meditating consistently on more and more of the Word hidden in the heart

Your word I have hidden in my heart, that I might not sin against You (Ps. 119:11). Let the words of my mouth and the meditation of my heart be acceptable in Your sight, O Lord, my strength and my Redeemer (Ps. 19:14).

W6.   Encountering Jesus in the Word for deepened transformation in Christlikeness

But we all, with unveiled face, … are being transformed into the same image from glory to glory, just as by the Spirit of the Lord (2 Cor. 3:18). If you abide in Me, and My words abide in you, you will ask what you desire, and it shall be done for you (Jn. 15:7). See also Lk. 24:32, Ps. 119:136, and 2 Cor. 1:20.

W7.   A life explained as one of "experiencing Scripture"

But this is what was spoken by the prophet Joel (Acts 2:16). This is my comfort in my affliction, for Your word has given me life (Ps. 119:50). My soul breaks with longing for Your judgements at all times (Ps. 119:20).

W8.   Living "naturally supernatural" in all of life as His Spirit makes the written Word (*logos*) the living Word (rhema)

So then aith comes by hearing, and hearing by the word (rhema) of God (Rom. 10:17). Your word is a lamp to my feet and a light to my path (Ps. 119:105).

W9.   Living abundantly "in the present" as His Word brings healing to hurt and anger, guilt, fear, and condemnation—which are heart hindrances to life abundant

"The thief does not come except to steal, and to kill, and to destroy" (Jn. 10:10). I will run the course of Your commandments, for You shall enlarge my heart (Ps. 119:32). "And you shall know the truth, and the truth shall make you free" (Jn. 8:32). Stand fast therefore in the liberty by which Christ has made us free, and do not be entangled again with a yoke of bondage (Gal. 5:1).

W10. Implicit, unwavering trust that His Word will never fail
"The grass withers, the flower fades, but the word of our God stands forever"
(Is. 40:8). *"So shall My word be that goes forth from My mouth; it shall not return
to Me void"* (Is. 55:11).

A SPIRIT-EMPOWERED DISCIPLE LOVES PEOPLE THROUGH

**P1. Living a Spirit-led life of doing good in all of life: relationships and
vocation, community and calling**
Who went about doing good ... (Acts 10:38). *"Let your light so shine before men,
that they may see your good works and glorify your Father in heaven"* (Mt. 5:16).
*"But love your enemies, do good, and lend, hoping for nothing in return; and your
reward will be great, and you will be sons of the Most High. For He is kind to the
unthankful and evil"* (Lk. 6:35). See also Rom. 15:2.

P2. "Startling people" with loving initiatives to "give first"
*"Give, and it will be given to you: good measure, pressed down, shaken together,
and running over will be put into your bosom"* (Lk. 6:38). *Then Jesus said, "Father,
forgive them, for they do not know what they do"* (Lk. 23:34). See also Lk. 23:43
and Jn. 19:27.

P3. Discerning the relational needs of others with a heart to give of His love
*Let no corrupt word proceed out of your mouth, but what is good for necessary
edification, that it might impart grace to the hearers* (Eph. 4:29). *And my God
shall supply all your need according to His riches in glory by Christ Jesus* (Phil.
4:19). See also Lk. 6:30.

P4.   Seeing people as needing BOTH redemption from sin AND intimacy in relationships, addressing both human fallen-ness and aloneness

But God demonstrates His own love toward us, in that while we were still sinners, Christ died for us (Rom. 5:8). *And when Jesus came to the place, He looked up and saw him, and said to him, "Zacchaeus, make haste and come down, for today I must stay at your house"* (Lk. 19:5). See also Mk. 8:24 and Gen. 2:18.

P5.   Ministering His life and love to our nearest ones at home and with family as well as faithful engagement in His body, the church

Husbands, likewise, dwell with them with understanding, giving honor to the wife, as to the weaker vessel, and as being heirs together of the grace of life, that your prayers may not be hindered (1 Pet. 3:7). See also 1 Pet. 3:1 and Ps. 127:3.

P6.   Expressing the fruit of the Spirit as a lifestyle and identity

But the fruit of the Spirit is love, joy, peace, longsuffering, kindness, goodness, faithfulness, gentleness, self-control (Gal. 5:22–23). *A man's stomach shall be satisfied from the fruit of his mouth; From the produce of his lips he shall be filled* (Prov. 18:20).

P7.   Expecting and demonstrating the supernatural as His spiritual gifts are made manifest and His grace is at work by His Spirit

In mighty signs and wonders, by the power of the Spirit of God, so that from Jerusalem and round about to Illyricum I have fully preached the gospel of Christ (Rom. 15:19). *"Most assuredly, I say to you, he who believes in Me, the works that I do he will do also"* (Jn. 14:12). See also 1 Cor. 14:1.

P8.   Taking courageous initiative as a peacemaker, reconciling relationships along life's journey

Be at peace among yourselves (1 Th. 5:13). *For He Himself is our peace, who has made both one, and has broken down the middle wall of separation* (Eph. 2:14). *Confess your trespasses to one another, and pray for one another, that you may be healed* (Jas. 5:16).

P9.   Demonstrating His love to an ever growing network of "others" as He continues to challenge us to love "beyond our comfort"
He who says, "I know Him," and does not keep His commandments, is a liar, and the truth is not in him (1 Jn. 2:4). If someone says, "I love God," and hates his brother, he is a liar; for he who does not love his brother whom he has seen, how can he love God whom he has not seen? (1 Jn. 4:20).

P10. Humbly acknowledging to the Lord, ourselves, and others that it is Jesus in and through us who is loving others at their point of need
"Take My yoke upon you and learn from Me, for I am gentle and lowly in heart, and you will find rest for your souls" (Mt. 11:29). "If I then, your Lord and Teacher, have washed your feet, you also ought to wash one another's feet" (Jn. 13:14).

A SPIRIT-EMPOWERED DISCIPLE LIVES HIS MISSION THROUGH

M1. Imparting the gospel and one's very life in daily activities and relationships, vocation and community
So, affectionately longing for you, we were well pleased to impart to you not only the gospel of God, but also our own lives, because you had become dear to us (1 Th. 2:8–9). See also Eph. 6:19.

M2.   Expressing and extending the kingdom of God as compassion, |justice, love, and forgiveness are shared
"I must preach the kingdom of God to the other cities also, because for this purpose I have been sent" (Lk. 4:43). "As You sent Me into the world, I also have sent them into the world" (Jn. 17:18). Restore to me the joy of Your salvation, and uphold me by Your generous Spirit. Then I will teach transgressors Your ways, and sinners shall be converted to You (Ps. 51:12–13). See also Mic. 6:8.

M3. Championing Jesus as the only hope of eternal life and abundant living

"Nor is there salvation in any other, for there is no other name under heaven given among men by which we must be saved" (Acts 4:12). *"The thief does not come except to steal, and to kill, and to destroy. I have come so that they may have life, and that they have it more abundantly"* (Jn. 10:10). See also Acts 4:12 and Jn. 14:6.

M4. Yielding to the Spirit's role to convict others as He chooses, resisting expressions of condemnation

"And when He has come, He will convict the world of sin, and of righteousness, and of judgment" (Jn. 16:8). *Who is he who condemns? It is Christ who died, and furthermore is also risen, who is even at the right hand of God, who also makes intercession for us* (Rom. 8:34). See also Rom. 8:1.

M5. Ministering His life and love to the "least of these"

"Then He will answer them saying, 'Assuredly, I say to you inasmuch as you did not do it to one of the least of these, you did not do it to Me' " (Mt. 25:45). *Pure and undefiled religion before God and the Father is this: to visit orphans and widows in their trouble, and to keep oneself unspotted from the world* (Jas. 1:27).

M6.   Bearing witness of a confident peace and expectant hope in God's lordship in all things

Now may the Lord of peace Himself give you peace always in every way. The Lord be with you all (2 Thess. 3:16). *And let the peace of God rule in your hearts, to which also you were called in one body; and be thankful* (Col. 3:15). See also Rom. 8:28 and Ps. 146:5.

M7.   Faithfully sharing of time, talent, gifts, and resources in furthering His mission

Of which I became a minister according to the stewardship from God which was given to me for you, to fulfill the word of God (Col. 1:25). *"For everyone to whom much is given, from him much will be required"* (Lk. 12:48). See also 1 Cor. 4:1–2.

M8.   Attentive listening to others' story, vulnerably sharing of our story, and a sensitive witness of Jesus' story as life's ultimate hope; developing your story of prodigal, preoccupied and pain-filled living; listening for others' story and sharing Jesus' story

But sanctify the Lord God in your hearts, and always be ready to give a defense to everyone who asks you a reason for the hope that is in you, with meekness and fear (1 Pet. 3:15). *"For this my son was dead and is alive again"* (Luke 15:24). See also Mk. 5:21–42 and Jn. 9:1–35.

M9.   Pouring our life into others, making disciples who in turn make disciples of others

"Go therefore and make disciples of all the nations, baptizing them in the name of the Father and of the Son and of the Holy Spirit, teaching them to observe all things that I commanded you; and lo, I am with you always, even to the end of the age" (Mt. 28:19–20). See also 2 Tim. 2:2.

M10. Living submissively within His body, the Church, as instruction and encouragement; reproof and correction are graciously received by faithful disciples

Submitting to one another in the fear of God (Eph. 5:21). *Brethren, if a man is overtaken in any trespass, you who are spiritual restore such a one in a spirit of gentleness, considering yourself lest you also be tempted* (Gal. 6:1). See also Gal. 6:2.

Notes

Notes

Notes